# Praise

'If you are concerned about the health and effectiveness of your organisation, *Good Culture* is an essential guide. The authors present an approach that defies many conventional management canons, with a basis instead in sound, systematic thinking rooted in academic Social Psychology and a consistent and well-established Philosophical value system. Their approach is evidenced and proven by extensive application in commerce, government and industry, and has been tested through practical experience. It will benefit organisations that strive to generate a culture of honesty, trust and social responsibility, and understand the value of a coherent approach.'

— **Professor Pat Langdon (PhD)**, Psychologist and Director, Transport Research Institute, Edinburgh Napier University

'Andrea Burns and Richard Davies have masterfully constructed an insightful and practical toolkit for the post pandemic world. This book is an essential guide to help companies and leaders build capabilities for today's and tomorrow's organisations to ensure ongoing business relevance and success. Built on solid experience and proven methods, the concepts are well constructed, easy to follow and will help CEOs, leadership and HR teams to focus on what really matters in people leadership, building teams and enabling an organisation to thrive. A fantastic read.'

— **Amanda Manzoni**, Chief Human Resources Officer, Ansell

'I have known, followed and benefitted from Andrea's sage counsel, personal and professional guidance and encouragement for the past fifteen years. It follows, therefore, that by digging deep into her considered and evidenced philosophies via this book, the reader will benefit, as will the culture and productivity of their outcomes. Thoroughly recommended.'

— **Commodore Phil Waterhouse**, Royal Navy

'Our diverse international and local workforce thrived in their teams after we invested in creating a venue team culture. *Good Culture* will reveal the most credible tool on the market so you too can get the best out of your team in today's new era of business.'

— **Anna Falconer**, International Major Event Consultant

'A truly insightful book for leaders wishing to create highly agile and adaptive organisations in the emerging new world of virtual working and unpredictable market events. Richard and Andrea have masterfully drawn on works by Maslow and Hartman to provide a step-by-step guide in creating Good Culture, together with real life examples, common pitfalls and tools, and, most importantly, how leaders need to "show up" to successfully take their people on this exciting and rewarding journey.'

— **Asada Harinsuit**, former Chairman, The Shell Companies, Thailand

'*Good Culture*, and the principles contained within, challenged my thinking and preconceptions. The methodology is completely logical and written in an engaging way, delivering real solutions to challenges with cultural strategies. It's a must-read for any individual looking to understand themselves better, and for leaders of any size team. Ultimately, this book is a structure for winning at life!'

— **Steve Hewitt**, Founder, 40 Percent and Profitunity

'Richard Davies and Andrea Burns have unlocked the secret for success in the increasingly digitalised, distributed, empowering, rapidly shifting world of business we all operate in – it's all about culture. *Good Culture* is a highly relevant read as it places re-tooled organisational culture at the heart of success in the modern workplace. I appreciated the authors' efforts in working through the why, what and all-important nine-step how-to for building the most appropriate culture from the ground up, with everyone involved and committed to the values and behaviours that define them and their organisation. This book is a blueprint for culture transformation in the modern workplace.'

— **Jeremy Blain**, CEO and international #1 best-selling author of *The Inner CEO: Unleashing leaders at all levels*

'I highly recommend *Good Culture* to leaders who are serious about understanding their people and adapting to new ways of working which make their businesses fit for purpose in the VUCA world. I believe that great responsibility rests on the shoulders of leaders to extend the adoption of good culture into the social stakeholder community, continuing its positive influence beyond working hours, which is increasingly important in the hybrid workplace, where work culture extends into the home.'

— **Pauline Norstrom FIoD FRSA**, Board Advisor (artificial intelligence and AFR), former Chair and honorary member, British Security Industry Association

'Andrea and Richard provide business leaders with a framework and clear pathway to achieving good culture. This book is an essential read for all current and aspiring business leaders who are focussed on creating a culture where talent is retained and people are happy and work together effectively in a high performance organisation.'

— **Richard J Bottomley OBE FCA**, FTSE 100 NED and former Senior Partner at KMPG

'*Good Culture* is a penetratingly insightful and practical toolkit for leaders committed to creating high performing teams of self-aware individuals. This leading edge "thinking styles" methodology successfully identifies, illuminates, inspires, measures and practically enables what Burns and Davies accurately pinpoint as the "cognitive diversity essential for innovation, strong decision making and good culture". Leaders committed to empowering, trusting and unlocking the potential within a team and accelerating the journey to success should read and act upon *Good Culture*.'

— **Captain Alistair Willis**, Royal Navy

'We learn from our mistakes, however, *Good Culture* will help you to avoid the worst of them, recover more swiftly and stay on a good path. It's an invaluable read as much for those setting out on their careers as it is for those who are well established in leadership.'

— **Stuart Burns**, CEO, Multi-Academy Trust

'This is an exceptionally well written philosophy of the relationships between Organisational Culture, Strategy, Value Science and the intrinsic links between them and the challenges that are posed by a new post COVID organisational operating environment in a VUCA world. Andrea and Richard have clearly captured the essence of the ultimate question, "What makes a good culture?" The comparison between Maslow's Hierarchical Theory of Needs and Dr Robert Hartman's Formal Axiology (Value Science) is a work of absolute genius.'

— **Steve Keogh**, CEO, ETM Associates Ltd

'The perfect blend of practical advice and proven theory, authored by seasoned operators with oodles of real-life experience to help you navigate and channel the beautiful diversity of human minds towards common objectives, *Good Culture* is the ultimate recipe book with all the ingredients you need to create something that everyone in your team can enjoy.'

— **Jonathan Skryme**, Chief of Staff, BiC

'*Good Culture* is a must-read for leaders in the post pandemic world. Andrea and Richard provide a practical, actionable process for how to keep teams engaged and performing at the top of their game – regardless of whether they're in-person, remote or hybrid workers. I know that my teams have some changes coming their way.'

— **Amy Lockmiller**, VP Communications,
Black & Decker

'As an early adopter of Axiometrics in England I am delighted to see the publication of this book. Value Science, and the tools of Formal Axiology, have allowed me to develop schools where an enabling culture is generated by deep values.'

— **David Brazier BA (Hons) MSC**, Headmaster, St James
Senior Boys School

'It doesn't matter how much business experience you have or what stage of the "journey" your business is at, getting a handle on culture is complex and challenging at times. Business owners with a desire to get a handle on culture and feel in control will benefit from reading this book. It will provide a sound and consistent framework within which to develop the culture you need to drive sustainable growth.'

— **Paul Aisthorpe**, CEO, ScaleAbility

*Good Culture* provides a toolkit of clear, effective and well proven pathways that will help businesses to move from a cultural aspiration to a positive cultural reality that benefits their teams, customers and financial performance.'

— **Dr Steve Bryce**, Founder, Catalytica

'If you truly care about the people and the values in your realm of responsibility, you need a quantifiable way to identify, track and achieve the goal of enhancing the 'good' in people. Good decision makers, placed in the right role, for the right reasons make great people. Great people create great cultures. Great cultures create great results. Leverage this framework and your people will thank you for it.'

— **Stephen Parker**, Project Parker Ltd

# GOOD
# CULTURE

Align your people,
profits and purpose
for the greater good

**Andrea Burns • Richard Davies**

# R<sup>e</sup>think

First published in Great Britain in 2022
by Rethink Press (www.rethinkpress.com)

Cover image © Ethan Daniels. Clear water covers a diverse reef in Wakatobi National Park off the southern coast of Sulawesi, Indonesia. Shutterstock

# Contents

# Introduction

2020 was a year of unprecedented change as we witnessed whole nations, cultures, organisations, businesses and people desperately transforming and evolving to survive in the face of the pandemic that threatened us all around the world. This process of transformation and revolution has persisted, as we continue to adjust to the new challenges posed by, and the novel problems of, the post-pandemic world. So much has changed, but how much should we really be looking to change back? Many changes occurred because they *had to*, but now is the time to pause and consider which of these changes we will keep because we *want to*. The pandemic forced us all to stop and review the existing and established ways of doing things. People have had more time to reflect on their lives, and many now require meaningful work that adds value beyond profit. Organisations have no choice but to move to meet their employees' demands and new expectations.

COVID-19 caused a monumental shift in ways of working that placed many knowledge workers at home overnight. Virtual and home working, historically subject to some stigma, was a trend growing gradually even before the pandemic, but overnight it became mainstream as governments around the world urged, and at times even ordered, people to stay at home. This dramatically accelerated the growth of globally distributed virtual teams, making it more critical than ever to adopt best practices to build good organisational cultures that work within our increasingly volatile, uncertain, complex and ambiguous world (VUCA). VUCA is an acronym first used in 1987 and coined by the US Army War College in the wake of the collapse of the USSR in the early 1990s;[1] it could not be more appropriate in a world where so much of what we knew and thought we understood is being called into question. We seem to be facing new threats on every side, as geopolitical, humanitarian, economic and environmental challenges grow. How can we, as business leaders, lead a steady course in such uncertain seas?

Certainty within our organisational structures and frameworks will help to provide stability. 'Strategy and culture are among the primary levers at top leaders' disposal in their never-ending quest to maintain organizational viability and effectiveness.'[2] The strategy provides the formal goals or objectives of an organisation for a long-term plan of action. Culture is more nebulous, much of it unspoken and intangible. It has been the subject of much academic research as people have tried time and again to define this abstract concept. It is experienced through the behaviours, actions, thoughts and social patterns of those within it; over time norms will develop within the group, and with that, expectations come about. There are Edgar Schein's 'artifacts', the 'espoused values and beliefs' and the 'basic underlying assumptions' within your organisation that become its habitat.[3] It is the environment in which activity occurs, driven and defined by the shared beliefs and values of those within it. It is 'the way things get done around here'.[4]

While strategy and culture are inextricably linked, there is a clear hierarchical relationship between the two:

> 'There is no more critical basis for business success or failure than the company's culture – it trumps strategy and leadership. That isn't to say that strategy doesn't matter, but rather that the particular strategy a company employs will succeed only if it is supported by the appropriate cultural attributes.'[5]

The observation is not that strategy is unimportant but simply that, however good the strategy, it is always the culture of a company that will determine its success. Culture is the human factor within an organisation, generated by those who work in it, particularly those who lead it. If the culture within an organisation is unhealthy, weak or poor, people will feel unfulfilled in their work. Organisations are only as good as their culture, and in the face of such growing volatility, this matters more than ever. This was confirmed by McKinsey & Company, in a study conducted in 2020, at the height of the pandemic:

'Organizations that focus on culture and organizational health accelerate out of a crisis faster. By building a performance culture with a unique set of practices, rituals, symbols, and experiences to fuel sustained superior performance, leaders can future-proof their organisations.'[6]

The absence of a healthy performance culture has seriously debilitating effects. Time and again research has demonstrated that around 70% of transformations and change programmes fail due to challenges relating to people and culture, and that 'when people are truly invested in change it is 30 percent more likely to stick.'[7] Culture matters. This was confirmed by the UK Corporate Governance Code which has, since 2018, stipulated that top companies must now publicly report on the application of the outlined cultural principles.[8]

Unfortunately, in our experience, it is far too common for leaders seeking to build high-performing organisations to be bewildered, intimidated and even hampered by the notion of addressing organisational culture. Indeed, many let it go unmanaged or make sporadic and faint-hearted attempts to launch superficial cultural initiatives; these may affect Schein's 'artifacts', but without addressing the deeper elements of culture, they fail to bring any lasting cultural change. Alternatively, some leaders diminish the idea of culture change such that it becomes little more than an HR function and a secondary concern for the organisation; but changing the personnel within an organisation will not transform the culture unless the other contributing elements are also addressed. Leaders may produce detailed analytical plans for strategy and execution, but these quickly go off the rails because the leaders have not understood culture's force, power and dynamics, and so they have failed to incorporate these elements into their plans. This is why management expert Peter Drucker is reported to have said 'culture eats strategy for breakfast.'[9] Strategy fails without appropriate consideration of culture.

How can organisations build a good culture in this rapidly evolving environment? Cultural change is usually a slow and sustained process that takes place over a long time, but the pandemic forced organisations to change their cultures overnight; as McKinsey proved, those with good agile cultures were able to achieve this most successfully and many who could not adapt did not survive. An immediate change was forced upon us all, and in times of crisis, people make remarkable adaptations. When change is known to be temporary, people can be accommodating, but what if some of these changes are to be permanent? How can we then put in place the necessary culture to support it?

One change that looks likely to remain is the shift towards a hybrid working model. The combination of having home-based and office-based workers provides the potential for increased innovation, performance and the ability to satisfy the needs of more potential clients. However, now that large portions of the workforce might be dotted across the map, it is more difficult than ever to build a good culture. Getting it right is important for all stakeholders, the personal well-being of staff, the quality of customer service and shareholder returns. The practical challenges are significant, but the potential rewards are huge.

We have written *Good Culture* because we are passionate about how to fix the culture crisis. Andrea, a leadership and productivity expert, is devoted to creating the necessary culture within a wide range of organisations that are committed to making a positive social impact that will enable them to deliver their vision and better outcomes that last for the people they serve. Previous clients include the Ministry of Defence (MOD), Waitrose and the National Health Service (NHS). She achieves this through her work at Catapult and Axiometrics® using insight gained through the application of Formal Axiology – an objective standard for measuring the structure and dynamics of a person's ability to make value judgements, as we shall discover in Part One. Richard has many years of experience in international commercial corporate roles where he discovered that his true passion was enabling and accelerating the personal development of individuals and improving the effectiveness and efficiency of teams. He was responsible for the training and development of half a million people in his last corporate role. He now coaches people to embed new skills and behaviour to improve their performance, increase focus and enhance business results. All individuals cited within this book have given permission to be included.

Together, we can help organisations develop the thinking agility so needed in the VUCA world and assist them to build the good organisational cultures necessary for the benefit of all. We also want to make more people aware of how the thinking of Abraham Maslow and Dr Robert Hartman has provided the foundation and tools required to build good cultures, and explain how this can be applied in practice.

Abraham Maslow (1908–1970) was an American psychologist who held academic positions at Columbia University, Brooklyn College, Brandeis University and finally, the Laughlin Institute in California. Maslow's lasting legacy is his development of the discipline of humanistic psychology – the study of good mental health, of which he considered we were all inherently capable. Sceptical of much of the earlier work on the human mind, Maslow was keen to identify the elements necessary for good mental health and true self-fulfilment, and his work therefore focuses not on viewing people as a 'bag of symptoms' or a bundle of problematic behaviours, but instead on identifying the positive qualities that motivate healthy individuals.[10] Within this humanistic approach, Maslow developed several theories that together laid the framework for much of the study in the field that followed.

Perhaps his most significant contribution is his idea of the 'Hierarchy of Needs', which we will discuss in detail in Chapter 2. At the top of his hierarchy is his concept of the 'self-actualising persons' – those who become all they can be are the most complete, fulfilled, conscientious, responsible, creative, compassionate, appropriately empathetic and most fully developed in their capacities and potentialities; in short, most fully human. This sounds like the type of leader we'll need in the challenging times ahead.

Maslow's work on human motivation heavily influenced and informed his colleague, contemporary and friend, Dr Robert Hartman (1910–1973). Hartman was born in Berlin but left in 1932 due to the rise of fascism and the growing strength of the Nazi movement in Germany, moving first to Europe, then to Mexico, before finally settling in the United States in 1941.[11] During his lifetime, he held many academic positions, including at Ohio State University, the Massachusetts Institute of Technology (MIT), Yale University, the National University of Mexico and the University of Tennessee. He was also a highly influential proponent of peace and in 1973 he was nominated for a Nobel Peace Prize; a significant volume of his essays and writings on war and peace was published in 2020.[12] We shall cover Hartman's work in detail throughout the book, but if you'd like to learn more about Hartman's life and work, we recommend that you read the autobiographical *Freedom to Live: The Robert Hartman story*, in which he tells the story of his life and explains his philosophy and science in more detail.[13]

As we will demonstrate in Chapter 2, there was a heavy degree of influence and collaboration between the two men, and we know that they often worked, and even holidayed, together.[14] In October 1957, Maslow and Hartman were the leading promoters of the First Scientific Conference on Knowledge and Human Values, held at MIT. From Maslow's seminal work on human values and their relationship to thought, Hartman then developed his concept of 'Formal Axiology or Value Science', enabling the ability 'to understand someone's "Structure of Thought" (the cause) meaning that their behaviour (the effect) can be predicted in any given situation.'[15] Hartman's work remains hugely influential in modern psychological study, and The Robert S Hartman Institute was established in 1976 'with the single intent of changing the world for the better through understanding the science of values.'[16] We are absolutely convinced that Hartman's Value Science offers the key to how organisations can build good agile cultures, as we shall demonstrate.

Hartman's Science of Value argues that behaviour can be predicted if the thinking driving it is understood. So to successfully change behaviour, it is key to understand the thinking behind it, leading to appropriately targeted initiatives. This contrasts with the many theories that attempt to build culture using behavioural-change initiatives. These approaches are founded on a fundamentally flawed assumption: that if individuals know how to do something, they will always do it, and that environment, culture or personal circumstance will have no impact on an individual's ability to perform as predicted; we know this is not the case. Initiatives focused on behaviour limit organisational competitive advantage and individual fulfilment.

They do not value the uniqueness of each team member, enable diversity of thought or harness their individual and collective innovative potential.

There is a commonly held albeit mistaken belief that behavioural-based psychometrics tools are accurate and objective, ie that their scores and findings are somehow arising from a comparison against some objective, external, fixed and quantifiable measures and that the results are therefore accurate, or approximate something close to it. However, these tests are inherently biased since they rely on people answering subjective questions about themselves. They rely on people's ability to know themselves accurately and to compare themselves objectively to others; it also assumes that respondents will be 100% honest with themselves when completing their questionnaires. Clearly, these are significant assumptions which in turn lead to notable limitations. As we shall see, this can also be said of 360-degree feedback methods, where the results will again be affected by the respondents' subjectivity and motivations, interrater variations and on whether feedback providers can fairly evaluate their colleagues' work attainment and organisational objectives. It assumes that participants have 'good' judgement, without understanding that cognitive ability, culture and personal circumstances all have a significant impact on judgement.

We know that the results of many of the standard psychometric and feedback assessment methods are inevitably and unavoidability affected by diversity, difference and interrater variability. However, we also know that these are some of the most valuable qualities to an organisation and therefore it is crucial that we can measure and quantify them. In *Good Culture*, we shall demonstrate how this cognitive diversity is essential for innovation, strong decision making and good culture. Organisations dominated by like-minded employees suffer from functional bias and low cognitive diversity, and results in the exclusion from the workplace of those who think differently.[17] Without an appropriate recognition and appreciation of different thinking patterns, teams quickly fall vulnerable to 'groupthink', and with this, the chance of common blind spots increases.[18] They miss the challenge from people who think and see things differently, and the result is weak decision making leading to poor performance. An organisation needs cognitive richness and flexible and accommodating thinking to survive, adapt and grow, but this diversity can only occur if the organisational culture is sufficiently good and healthy.

In *Good Culture*, we will introduce and explain the steps and elements necessary to create a good culture, arranged in two sections. Section One investigates the *Why*: why developing a good culture is so important, and why now is the time to build a good organisational structure as individuals, leaders and organisations begin to move beyond the challenges of the pandemic that they have been grappling with since March 2020. We shall introduce some major concepts from the work of Maslow and Hartman and also explain why Value Science (Formal Axiology) can provide the tools and methodology needed to build cognitive capacity and thinking diversity, improve decision making and build a structurally robust culture to meet the challenges, now and tomorrow.

Section Two, the *How*, sets out the 9 Performance Pathways necessary to define and build the good culture necessary for all organisations, whether office-based, hybrid or virtual. These pathways, informed by Hartman's principles, are a series of nine distinct, ordered steps that need to be worked through and applied from the first to the last, in the process acquiring the skills and strategies required to develop a good culture. Our 9 Performance Pathways are:

1. Building Trust and the Common Bond

2. Building Team Synergy

3. Setting Vision, Mission and Purpose

4. Instilling Responsibility and Integrity

5. Getting Results

6. Developing Strategies and Discipline

7. Fostering Innovation and Change

8. Preparation and Tactics

9. Maintaining Consistency and Conformity

Work through these pathways in sequence and you will have established the good culture you need and developed the ability to sustain it.

## TOOL: GOOD CULTURE SCORE CARD

 Before heading into the rest of the book, we'd like to give you some food for thought about your current culture. You can get a free snapshot of your culture by taking our good culture scorecard. It will give you an instant risk assessment of the health of your culture (high/low or medium). You can then dive deeper with our second scorecard to help you diagnose the pain points that may be damaging your culture. Scan the QR code or follow the link: *https://good-culture.scoreapp.com*

# SECTION ONE
## THE WHY

# 1
# The Case For An Agile Culture

## Why is agile culture important?

Our world has changed. The VUCA world of constant change and turbulence is here to stay, and navigating this 'permanent white water' requires a different approach to ensuring organisational success.[19]

The humanitarian and economic crises triggered by the pandemic enforced rapid, radical change in business. It drove a mass unplanned social experiment with millions forced to work remotely almost overnight. Companies had to adapt their models and operations and the stigma of working from home diminished. People had time to reflect, and many now demand meaningful work that adds value beyond profit. Retention is likely to become more complex. The hybrid working model emerged, ie part office-based working and part remote, and for many of us, the daily commute came to an end. All this change is exhausting; a study by Gartner published in October 2021 noted that '54% of HR leaders say their employees are fatigued from all the change.'[20]

In the introduction, we noted the persuasive financial argument in favour of a healthy workplace culture. How do we define a 'good' or 'healthy' culture, and how can we create one? This book will use Hartman's 9 Performance Pathways as a way to identify and define a 'good culture', which we will explore across nine chapters. We will then consider the steps and elements necessary to create such a culture. Before this, there is one crucial factor that we must consider: agile decision making. We believe that if people throughout an organisation can make swift, good-quality decisions, this will lead to better outcomes and higher performance.

## Agility is not a behaviour

Organisations that put a focus on behaviours are getting it wrong. Imagine a CEO asking employees to demonstrate agile behaviour; how would that look? People swerving around desks as they navigate the office? Home-based colleagues touching their toes while conversing on Zoom? Think about it: do you 'behave' your way out of a crisis? No, we *think* our way through challenges.

Behavioural-change programmes don't work. They don't focus on creating the right conditions, making good decisions or enabling correct behaviours. People are not consistent in their behaviour. Imagine a company programme that prescribed a specific set of customer-service sales behaviours and required employees to send in their sales proposals by a precise date and time. A behavioural-change programme is trialled, and as a result, the expectation is now that the employees will meet these stipulations 100% of the time. Now imagine a salesperson who has recently returned from that programme: earlier that week, they had promised to send a proposal to a client by 5pm on Friday. A colleague pops by and announces that it's pub time and the drinks are on them. In these circumstances, do you think there's a chance that the salesperson will skip the proposal writing and go to the pub? Of course! It is free will in action. The training programme prescribed a particular set of rules and values but did not consider whether participants were likely to value and act upon the course content. Behaviour-based programmes don't consider the risk of team members ignoring the required behaviours and instead are based upon a flawed expectation of 100% compliance. It also assumes that the culture enables the right behaviour to be selected. It does not allow for good or bad judgement or free will.

Think about it: just because somebody has been told a particular behaviour is expected, does this then guarantee their action when given a choice? Furthermore, we cannot ensure absolute consistency of message; every individual thinks differently, with their own inherent beliefs and experiences, so everybody will both bring and take away something different from a training programme. People presented with the same learning materials will still see it through their own eyes, focusing on some things, ignoring others and interpreting it as they see fit. This individuality cannot be controlled or eradicated but must instead be acknowledged and accommodated when planning change.

The impact of this individuality can be explained and explored through Hartman's Science of Value, which explains the natural order of things and is introduced in the following chapter. As you will learn, Formal Axiology is the study of these values, and by using axiological tools, we can come to understand the likely impact of these individual thinking preferences and values and therefore better predict the decisions that may result. It's all about understanding the thinking behind the way individuals make decisions, and how cognitive ability creates mental agility. Creating an agile culture requires a methodology that understands and harnesses cognitive diversity – the organisation's thinking capital.

## A culture of agility

Agility addresses volatility. Leaders and workers at all levels need to have the ability to make the right decisions, understand and mitigate risk in their environment, and maintain trust and reputation in our ever-changing world. People and organisations require unprecedented flexibility and need to adapt quickly to change, frequently needing to make decisions in real time. These attributes are directly related to the talent and decision-making capabilities of the individuals and can make or break organisational success. As Johansen has noted, 'Organisations successful in a VUCA world are very clear about where they are going, yet very flexible about how they are getting there.'[21]

Imagine an organisation where each person fulfils their full potential as a person in all its manifestations. This state of self-fulfilment is represented by 'self-actualisation' in Maslow's famous 'Hierarchy of Human Needs' model, at the top of his five-level pyramid as described in 1943,[22] and just below 'transcendence' in his expanded seven-level pyramid of 1964 (to be considered in Chapter 2).[23] We describe such organisations as having a 'Blue Ocean' culture, a concept coined by W Chan Kim and Renée Mauborgne, implying a culture free of competition and contest, in stark contrast to the 'Red Ocean' cultures of shark-infested waters bloodied by infighting, low trust and low engagement.[24] How do you think such an organisation would feel and perform?

The days of consultation up and down the chain of command are gone. With increased remote and hybrid working patterns, many workers have lost the ability to ask around the office for advice and pointers or to pop by somebody's desk for a quick chat. Leaders must be confident that they have communicated directions effectively and unambiguously, and that their team members feel empowered to solve problems independently and use their initiative. It's not easy for a leader to gauge actual levels of trust and commitment when many of their team members are dotted across the map.

The good news is that a hybrid model can create a more inclusive culture, enabling a greater diversity of thought. People who prefer working from home will now bring more of their thinking capital to their job than when they had to work in an office environment where they felt less comfortable; research shows that introverts and the 'quiet deliverers' who previously flew under the radar in a hectic office often flourish when working remotely.[25] Conversely, those who prefer working in an office can thrive by continuing to do so. This combination of both home-based and office-based workers provides the potential for increased innovation and performance, and the ability to satisfy the needs of more potential clients.

The theory of a blue ocean, high trust, harmonious hybrid culture is appealing, but the practical hurdles in attaining such a culture are significant. Mutual trust throughout the organisation is key, but achieving it can be a real challenge.

## Why remote working can fail

'Proximity bias' is a natural phenomenon that can be observed as a by-product of remote working. The BBC describes it as 'an unconscious – and unwise – tendency to give preferential treatment to those in our immediate vicinity' and notes how destructive this subconscious long-term favouritism can become.[26] It can significantly impair the quality of meetings and decisions, as leaders and organisations seek to generate instantaneous and innovative reactions to the rapidly changing world of the pandemic and beyond. When an immediate response is required, leaders tend to turn first to the most readily available resources – those who are closest. The time and effort required to schedule a meeting with remote workers can appear to waste valuable brainstorming and problem-solving time, but by choosing not to make this time, they inadvertently exclude the expertise of remote workers.

It gets worse. Research shows that we look more favourably on those we see more often. Employees with physical proximity to their team leaders can be seen as better workers and ultimately find more success than their remote counterparts, while the skills and the expertise of those further away are often undervalued. It's a corporate case of, in a hurry, 'out of sight, out of mind'.

Failure to address proximity bias will limit organisations. Leaders need to take conscious steps to mitigate this, working to ensure that remote workers are fully included and remain on track for promotions. They also need to understand the unique thinking capability of their people, to maximise their potential and to avoid isolated remote workers leaving to join more inclusive employers, robbing the organisation of their underappreciated and unharnessed talent.

An inability to cultivate trust effectively among remote team members is the root cause of many organisations' failure. When everyone worked in the office, the seeds of trust were often planted without us even being aware – a greeting in the lift, post-meeting small talk, complimenting a colleague's haircut or a chat over the coffee machine. With hybrid and remote working, leaders have had to find new ways to facilitate the building of this trust between employees. If this is not done, the results can be catastrophic: a 2020 study by Gartner revealed that 'only 44% of employees say they trust their organization's leaders and managers to navigate a crisis well.'[27] In the uncertain post-pandemic world, this is a sobering statistic.

When there is low or no trust between members and within an organisation, this can result in significant lost value and potential. Those team members further removed from the 'proximal' core – those working remotely or in a hybrid model – may feel too uncertain or afraid to share their true opinions and express their views openly. If they do muster the courage to speak up, their colleagues will often ignore them as they don't want to validate the input of one now seen more as a competitor than as a remote colleague; this reinforces the remote worker's sense of being undervalued, excluded and 'unfavoured'. This is a highly destructive and reductive process, as further divisions leave people increasingly disillusioned and dissatisfied by their role within the organisation, diminishing trust and cohesion yet further. If people feel unable to express their authentic perspectives or find that others won't listen to them if they do, the potential value to the organisation that they can each contribute is lost. When divergent thinking is not invited, offered or received, decision making suffers; poor decisions produce poor performance. Establishing a solid foundation of mutual trust throughout an organisation is therefore fundamental to establishing an agile culture.

It does not end there. The remote team leader faces yet more challenges. A scattered workforce requires new approaches to the classic leadership problems: how to create team synergy; instil responsibility and integrity; deliver results; create a successful strategy; foster innovation and change; ensure good preparation and establish conformity. The old solutions often relied on close physical proximity, ongoing oversight and supervision, and immediate access to team members, whether to brainstorm projects together or to address possible issues before they developed into problems to be resolved. New strategies for how to address each of these problems need to be identified.

Conflict within a virtual team is much more testing for leaders to resolve than conflict within an office-based group. Richard knows all about this; he has eighteen years of experience working in corporate virtual teams and has worked with the good, the bad and the ugly. In remote teams, a cocktail of low trust, isolation and heightened emotions invariably fuels conflict. This conflict may not be overt – it often simmers beneath the veneer of hollow team conference call 'camaraderie'. Our social glue comes from the small incidental conversations and observations that develop our sense of a shared humanity and the relationships between us; without this, ensuring a cohesive team can be much harder.

Trust is easier to build when we physically spend time together. This makes it much easier to read the nonverbal cues of your colleagues and better assess their meaning, and provides numerous almost intangible opportunities to check in with each other, quickly clearing up misunderstandings before tensions escalate. This places hybrid or remote workers at a disadvantage compared to their office-based colleagues. Their only contact with their colleagues may be via audio or video call, and while these online meetings do replicate many of the characteristics of an in-person meeting, they also pose some unique challenges for the workers attending virtually.

Unlike being in a shared space, homeworkers cannot read the body language of the on-screen heads and shoulders of their on-screen colleagues and can struggle to assess the tone and timbre of the meeting. Those attending a meeting virtually know that their contact with their colleagues is limited in both time and location; there are no opportunities for building that social glue. They may become acutely aware of their exclusion from the experiences shared by their colleagues before the call and those that will continue after; they may hear 'in-jokes' from their office-based colleagues, or puzzle at references to an earlier conversation in the corridor, or an event in the canteen. Their physical separation from their colleagues is almost mirrored in the social isolation that results from being additionally excluded from the shared office-based experiences and culture. As humans, we have a natural tendency to fear the unknown, so these moments when the virtual colleagues feel excluded from the knowledge apparently shared by others can quickly breed fear and anxiety, again reducing mutual trust. These challenges have all taken on new weight in an era of virtual interactions, magnified dramatically by the enforced isolation and anxiety generated by the pandemic.

## Nine barriers to building an agile culture in a virtual world

We list nine elements of remote and hybrid working that can hamper the ability of organisations to build trust and attain an agile culture.

1. **Knowledge sharing.** Too often, valuable knowledge resides only in specific people's heads, and many organisations do not systematically capture or codify this wisdom to share across the workforce. Companies have instead relied solely upon informal and sometimes unreliable methods of transmitting and distributing this information, such as by employees tapping their colleagues on the shoulder to ask a question, or sharing a coffee to learn from their insight, experience and knowledge. Virtual working and geographically dispersed teams make it difficult to foster relationships across their team and to facilitate this informal and somewhat haphazard distribution of knowledge.

2. **Socialisation.** People can feel isolated and disconnected from their colleagues and the organisation when they work remotely. When some of their colleagues are sharing the same workspace while they remain alone at home, this further exacerbates the feeling of isolation for the remote workers who feel excluded from the informal information flow of the office. In short, it makes it difficult to foster relationships between colleagues.

3. **Camaraderie.** Another concern of hybrid working is that the quality of peer-to-peer relationships deteriorates due to the lack of in-person contact. People can't bump into each other when they are miles apart, and it removes the opportunity for natural small talk and the observation of incidental social cues. The virtual world makes it nearly impossible for leaders to observe, encourage and maintain relationships across their teams. Without frequent in-person encounters, managers may miss early signs of burnout, disengagement, relationship breakdowns or team dysfunction. They can't see as many social cues and may struggle to get a clear 'read' on the other person's state of mind when they can only see them via their 'Zoom face'.

4. **Mentoring.** Mentoring relationships require deep mutual trust and a strong interpersonal relationship. For some people, their strengths lie elsewhere and they may struggle to strike up a rapport and establish trust readily; others have clarity, a natural focus on empathy, and build relationships with others quickly

and easily. How can the development of this deep trust be facilitated and fostered when people only see each other on screen?

5. **Recruitment.** The growing trend towards the use of personality and behavioural psychometrics in recruitment is problematic, with ongoing concerns around reliability and validity. Psychometric testing requires an individual to answer a long set of questions about themselves to provide the questioner with increased knowledge of their psychology from which they can better predict that individual's behaviour. There are obviously significant limitations to this. How well do people know themselves? Do they always provide wholly truthful answers, or might they be tempted to second-guess the answers they think their prospective employer wants to hear? Can the study of personality reliably be used to predict behaviour, and even if it can, do those predictions hold just as true within the workplace? Blinkhorn and Johnson believe not: 'There is little evidence of enduring relationships between personality test scores and measures of success at work.'[28] Use of psychometric testing when recruiting for a virtual or hybrid working model is even less well established, and it is likely that quite different parameters will need to be used to predict a potential employee's likely success as a remote or hybrid worker.

6. **Collaboration and innovation.** If you don't have a high level of trust within a team, collaboration and innovation will suffer. People will be reluctant to share

their ideas or 'brainwaves' if they do not trust others, perhaps because they are concerned others could steal them and claim them as their own, or perhaps because they fear judgement or ridicule. Hybrid working also removes all the opportunities for unplanned interactions when people bump into each other in the corridor or canteen; these spontaneous and informal gatherings increase social cohesion and strengthen relationships, and the resulting conversations often spark collaboration and innovation that gives birth to new ideas. Steve Jobs considered the serendipity of such random meetings to be so vital that he specifically designed the Pixar Animation building to maximise such unplanned meetings and interactions, and thereby encourage the creative and spontaneous collaboration that would so often result.[29]

7. **Onboarding.** Onboarding is the process of showing new joiners 'how to do things around here' and what they need to do in their new role; they are also indoctrinated in the company's vision, history, processes and culture. Some aspects of the onboarding process – such as essential written information or company documentation – can be sent out for remote consumption. However, other aspects of the induction and integration process – such as gaining an appreciation of the company's culture, mores and unspoken expectations – are much harder to achieve virtually. Historically, coming to understand these more intangible elements of the onboarding process has required numerous face-to-face interactions and encounters with existing employees, accustomed

to having those conversations in person; trying to complete these processes virtually requires significant adaptation and modification by all concerned. Opportunities for on-the-job observation are severely restricted and it can be harder for new remote workers to build the trust bonds required for them to feel confident enough to ask 'stupid' questions of their supervisor, buddy or remote colleagues. The pandemic forced the entire global workforce to undertake a mass shift towards a work-from-home model, and this enabled some unprecedented opportunities to study the impact of remote and hybrid working patterns. According to a PricewaterhouseCoopers (PwC) survey conducted nine months into the work-from-home shift in the USA, employees with the least professional experience 'need the office the most' and are 'more likely to want to be in the office more often', where they can more readily take advantage of their more experienced colleagues and managers.[30] The entire onboarding process will need to be revised and reimagined to address these additional challenges.

8. **Performance evaluation.** It is challenging to avoid proximity bias when some members work in the office while others work from their homes, whether flexibly or permanently. When a supervisor rarely gets to see a team member in person or observe them working, how can they ensure they are giving them equal treatment and being fully inclusive? How can they make objective decisions about how well the remote worker behaves and performs when the criteria used

to judge them against their office-based colleagues are so different?

9. **Data security.** Ensuring the security of data outside the office poses a long list of new challenges: security of domestic Wi-Fi; sharing across public networks; safe storage of information and so on. Cyber security has been a growing threat that organisations have long been struggling to combat, but the pandemic brought about, almost overnight, an immense rise in the number of people working from home and accessing work from their own devices. This has monumentally increased the risks and challenges.

While remote and hybrid working undoubtedly poses some additional difficulties in the creation of a workplace trust culture, we have seen a deeply concerning trend among various companies towards the adoption of solutions that seem worryingly regressive and counterproductive. Where mutual trust has not already been established, some of today's anxious managers are resorting to surveillance techniques to ensure maximal staff productivity; we call this 'digital piecework'. Technology is being introduced into their employees' own homes expressly to spy on them: some employers have started to use software to track workers' keystrokes, mouse clicks and website history; some take screenshots of employees to check that they are at their screens; some even use webcam software to monitor eye movements and facial expressions. The information provided through these surveillance methods is then checked against a worker's output to monitor their productivity. Perhaps unsurprisingly, evidence demonstrates that the use of such techniques make people feel vulnerable, afraid and less creative.[31] These 'surveillance managers' drain job satisfaction and destroy morale, and the culture of suspicion and doubt that they create stands in direct opposition to a culture of trust. Trust is a two-way street; if the leaders don't trust staff, why should teams trust their leaders? We know that without trust, creativity and progress will stall; employees will not have the confidence to risk taking initiative or making powerful decisions for fear of possible repercussions or negative consequences. It is an appalling abdication of leadership to fail to build trust.

## Summary

A culture of trust that supports agile decision making facilitates better outcomes faster. If you can ensure these optimal conditions exist, up and down the organisation, it will lead to better outcomes and performance. However, as we have outlined in this chapter, it is not easy. There are many barriers to overcome, especially now that hybrid and remote working has become mainstream. We know that behavioural-based change or culture programmes are not the answer. If your habit is to reach for the familiar psychometric tools expecting the results to underpin a behavioural-change programme, stop! These are more akin to horoscopes. In the next chapter, we'll bust some myths about psychometric tools.

We conclude this chapter by posing two questions. Are you committed and equipped to create a rigorous culture of trust and agile thinking within your organisation? Are you ready and prepared to deal with the unforeseen challenges and opportunities that such a future will bring?

What if you could create an agile culture where mutual trust is high across your organisation, and you have eliminated proximity bias? The result is that you could be confident that people will do the right thing and consistently make good decisions. What if you could reduce overall bias? What if you could find a proven way to build trust and build team synergy? What if you could create a good culture to connect remote and office-based workers? Good news: the rest of this book does just that, as it introduces a framework and supplies the tools to make it possible.

In Chapter 2, we will provide a proper introduction to Value Science, or Axiology as it is also known, and the associated Axiometrics® tools. The following nine chapters will then explain each of Hartman's 9 Performance Pathways and demonstrate how they offer a blueprint for building a good organisational culture that enables agility.

# 2
# Value Science – The Natural Order Of Things

A xiology, or the 'theory of value', is the philosophical concept behind 'the study of goodness, or value, in the widest sense of these terms.'[32] While initially its use was confined to economics, used generally to indicate the 'value' of an object – its financial worth – it then began to be applied more widely to mean the philosophical study of values, whether they be moral, aesthetic, religious, political, scientific or cultural.

In 1967, Robert Hartman published his seminal work, *The Structure of Value*, in which he applied the tools of reason, logic and mathematics to the philosophical 'theory of values' to develop a new frame of reference – the Science of Values.[33] This Formal Axiology is heavily grounded in scientific practice and techniques and enables numerical analysis of the 'value' of things as well as objects. It is a unique social science because it is the only social science that has a one-to-one relationship between a field of mathematics (transfinite mathematical sets) and its dimensions.[34] This robust methodology can then be used to define the things that people consider to have value, such as personality and culture, and also provides a mathematical framework with which we can measure the success of a thing: 'a thing is good insofar as it exemplifies its concept.'[35] This can even be utilised to quantify concepts as abstract as leadership success and team capacities.

---

 If you would like to watch a short video to find out more about the origins of Axiology and Axiometrics®, scan the QR code or follow this link: *www.catapult-solutions.co.uk/the-origins-of-axiology-and-axiometrics*

---

In this chapter, we provide a basic introduction to Axiology and Axiometrics®. We position these metrics within the context of conventional psychometrics introduce the nine pathways which we use to define a 'good' culture in the following nine chapters of the book.

## What is culture?

If we wish to measure culture, we will first have to define it. McKinsey & Company provided an excellent definition of culture in a recent podcast: 'When we think about culture, we think about a standard set of behaviors, plus the underlying mindsets that shape how people work and interact day to day.'[36] However, not only does this podcast define culture, but it also outlines how fundamental it is to any organisation that this corporate foundation is solid, shared and wholesome: 'What we see in the data is compelling: companies with healthy cultures have three times greater total returns to shareholders.' We noted in the introduction how over two-thirds of cultural change programmes fail,[37] too often because they haven't first undertaken the right steps 'to change mind-sets and behavior', ie the culture of the organisation.[38] That's a sobering statistic.

So what does this mean for leaders? To face the challenges of a hybrid working world, leaders need to ensure the 'mind-sets and behavior' of their employees are healthy, flexible and committed, keeping the culture healthy and helping their people to be the best they can be, regardless of whereabouts in the world they might be sitting.

## Let's start with Maslow

We touched upon Abraham Maslow in the introduction. He is best known for his 1943 paper, 'A theory of human motivation', in which he outlined his hierarchy of the various needs that motivate human behaviour.[39] According to Maslow's model (used also in his 1954 book, *Motivation and Personality*),[40] people have five levels of needs, each of which must be met if they are to fully realise their potential:

1. **Physiological needs:** Food, water, sleep

2. **Safety needs:** Of body, of employment, of resources

3. **Love and belonging needs:** Friendship, intimacy, familial relationships

4. **Esteem needs:** Confidence, achievement, self-respect, respect from others

5. **Self-actualisation:** Morality, creativity, the ability to problem solve

These five levels are often pictured as a pyramid, with the universal needs of society (the physiological needs) at the base, rising through the levels towards the highest state of psychological development (self-actualisation). According to Maslow's theory, people can only move up a level once the needs of the lower level have been fulfilled. For example, somebody who isn't getting enough sleep won't have met the needs of the lowest level so they could never reach the highest level, that of self-actualisation, the state of achieving absolute personal self-realisation: 'the desire to become more and more what one is, to become everything that one is capable of becoming.'[41]

Maslow continued to refine and develop his hierarchy of needs throughout his life, producing a series of publications to advance the theory. In his 1971 book *The Farther Reaches of Human Nature*, Maslow acknowledged that his preferred way of both thinking and speaking about self-actualisation 'was suggested to me about fifteen years ago by the axiological writings of Hartman, who defined "good" as the degree to which an object fulfils its definition or concept'.[42] To be 'good', a person had to be fully self-fulfilled – Maslow's self-actualisation.

Influenced by Hartman's Science of Value and the idea of higher levels of psychological fulfilment, Maslow later expanded his hierarchy of 'deficiency needs' to include the 'growth needs', first adding cognitive and aesthetic needs,[43] and then later incorporating an eighth level of need, with one further state (transcendence) which sits above the pyramid.[44]

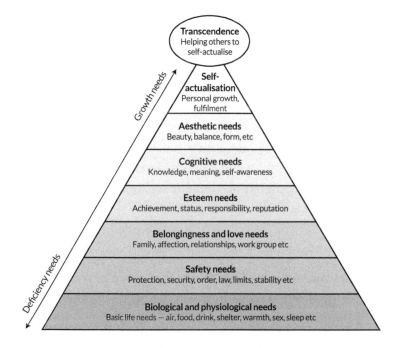

**Source:** Adapted from Maslow, A H, *Religions, Values, and Peak Experiences* (Penguin, 1970, original work published 1964)

**Cognitive needs** describe our need to know and acquire relevant knowledge and the skills required to function efficiently and effectively; also our ability to contribute to society and to face the numerous everyday challenges in our environment. In other words, every day's a school day. It is our curiosity and our need for exploration, but matched by a desire for predictability, meaning and understanding; if we want to keep up with the pace of change, we need to embrace lifelong learning. The pyramid also describes cognitive needs as 'self-awareness' – an understanding of our own intrinsic strengths/vulnerabilities.

**Aesthetic needs** describe the need to enjoy and promote the beauty of the environment, both natural and artificial. It's about the appreciation of our scenery and art in society. This is an intrinsic need and something that we feel, not something that we need.

**Self-transcendence** sits above the expanded seven-level pyramid. This is not a widely considered concept. It's open to various interpretations, but the following are core characteristics of self-transcendent people:

- They must already have achieved self-actualisation.

- They are motivated by values that move beyond the personal self to focus more on the needs of others.

- This desire to help others becomes their motivation, perhaps even driving them to focus solely on factors that do not impact them but others.

- Their motivations may appear to transcend time and culture and, therefore, they are able to consider things from a broad angle, free of self-interest or personal limitations.

- Such people are driven less by extrinsic motivation – arising from external factors, such as the desire for external reward or to receive something from someone else.

- Instead, they are driven more by intrinsic motivation – they seek internal pleasure and are driven by a desire to generate personal satisfaction.

## What makes us good?

We have already considered one area in which Maslow was heavily influenced by Robert Hartman. Growing from his hierarchy of needs, Maslow's work moved in his later years to consider what feeds the human soul, ie what are the core beliefs that make a person who they are. Maslow gave particular credit to Hartman for providing a methodological scientific approach to measuring values, which he was able to use to develop his theory of the values of being.[45] These Being-values (B-values) were fundamental to his work on studying the meta motivation behind everything we think and do, as explored in his Being-psychology or B-psychology. Maslow's *Toward a Psychology of Being* was published in 1962. More than 200,000 copies of the book were sold in the first few years.

The language of self-realisation and personal growth perspectives permeated the university environment and fed the counterculture of the 1960s, and is now widely established within the world of business.

Hartman's concept of value as a measurement of the extent to which a thing realises its true potential or 'exemplifies its concept' – Maslow's notion of self-actualisation – requires that these Being-values are first identified. Hartman proposed four questions that an individual must ask themselves to identify their personal B-values that give their life and work meaning:

- What am I here for in the world?
- Why do I work for this organisation?
- What can this organisation do to help me fulfil my meaning in the world?
- How can I help this organisation help me fulfil my meaning in the world?[46]

Hartman's work gave us a framework to enable people to achieve Maslow's self-actualisation, and this process underpins the 9 Performance Pathways needed to build a good culture which we will cover in Section Two of this book. At the core of this lies Hartman's Three Dimensions of Value.

# Hartman's Three Dimensions of Value

Hartman's lifelong quest was to find an answer to one fundamental question, 'What is good?' Using that answer, good could then be systematised and organised, whether that be good within an organisation, person, idea, political system, meal or a job. Not only could 'good' be identified and organised, but it is also a value that can be measured: 'The value of anything is determined by the extent to which it meets the intension of its concept.'[47]

Hartman's conception of 'good' as a definable and measurable value has meant that, by using the same mathematical framework to define it, we can come to understand how an individual sees and values things within their world that will subsequently drive their behaviour. Hartman established a usable and testable scientific method to order value, based on transfinite mathematical sets, and the mathematical and logical structure of value concepts is the cornerstone of Axiology. He also developed a method method to understand what orders our moral decisions and value judgements, and enables us, at last, to understand.

## Why do we do what we do?

To think about how an individual would answer this question, Hartman devised a way to break down every evaluation into three specific value dimensions: intrinsic, extrinsic and systemic. Everything is valued in one or more of these three ways that can be identified philosophically and mathematically.

1. **Intrinsic dimension:** Unique to humans, the intrinsic value of the self

2. **Extrinsic dimension:** Actions, things as they exist in the world

3. **Systemic dimension:** Ideas, thoughts, intellect

There are therefore three forms of value, but also three forms of valuation. For example, to feel love is an intrinsic valuation, but it can be applied towards an idea (a systemic value), a thing (an extrinsic value) or a person (an intrinsic value).

The beauty of Hartman's dimensions is their universality. For example, consider the classical triad of beauty, truth and wisdom, the three transcendentals of medieval thought. Metaphysics argues these are the fundamental properties of being, and therefore common to all beings. As this table demonstrates, the three value dimensions have formed the foundation of a vast range of fields of studies and intellectual endeavour.

| Applied to: | Intrinsic value | Extrinsic value | Systemic value |
| --- | --- | --- | --- |
| Individual persons | Ethics | Psychology | Physiology/ Neuroscience |
| Groups of persons | Political Science, Social Ethics | Sociology | Law of Persons |
| Individual things | Aesthetics | Economics | Technology |
| Groups of things | Civilisation | Ecology | Civil Engineering, Law of Property, Industrial Technology, Ritual, Games |
| Concepts | Metaphysics | Epistemology | Logic |
| Words | Poetry | Rhetoric | Grammar |

# The Hartman Value Profile

Having established a science and a methodology for how to measure value, Hartman then created an assessment tool to enable the practical application of his scientific methods within the field of psychology. The Hartman Value Profile was therefore developed to measure the character of an individual and to form an objective assessment of their thinking pattern against logical, mathematical norms.

To complete an HVP, a person is assessed across three core thinking dimensions, and in relation to their specific blend of self and world thinking processes:

1. **Intuitive thinking (people):** The thinking we use when we connect, bond, or identify with or 'get inside' our subject (usually other people); our gut instincts and feelings; the ability to understand, appreciate and see value, both in ourselves and in others; empathy and an unconditional acceptance of the other's uniqueness, without evaluating, judging or critiquing.[48]

   An example of this could be connecting with someone so deeply that you feel a resonance with that person; time spent together seems to fly and yet you may not be able to tell me what they were wearing. Another example is being so involved in a project that one doesn't even notice that an hour or two has passed. This thinking is intrinsic.

2. **Pragmatic thinking (task):** The thinking required for real-world considerations, in real time; paying attention to properties, parts and steps; measuring, weighing, comparing and processing the environment. This thinking is extrinsic.

3. **Conceptual thinking (systems):** The thinking we use when focusing on rules, order, meaning, plans, goals, the future and ideas; 'black and white' thinking; working within established principles and standards.

# The Three Dimensions of Value

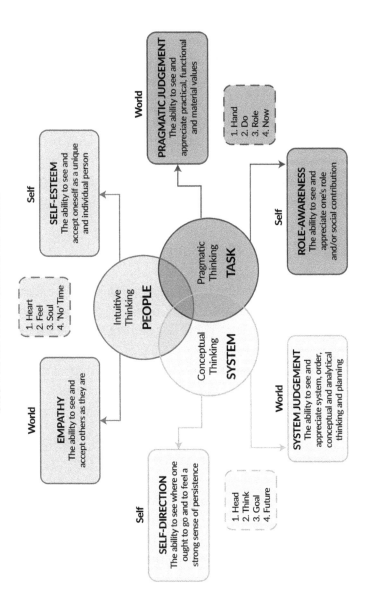

This is the ability to focus on the object, seeing it not from within, not on the surface but from 'outside' the object and at a distance; the ability to see and understand an idea or concept; a commitment to the inner self. This thinking is systemic.

Let's take a deeper look at these thinking patterns and consider how they can manifest in the workplace. To bring this to life, let me ask you to think about your colleagues; can you identify colleagues whose dominant thinking style illustrates each of Hartman's thinking dimensions?

## The intuitive thinker (people)

Have you noticed how some colleagues are 'all about the people'? These people's thinking is heavily focused on the intrinsic dimension. Their decision making is influenced by considerations of others: What will other people think? How will they feel? What is the potential impact on clients, colleagues and stakeholders? Some colleagues might consider these people to be a bit 'soft and fluffy'.

## The pragmatic thinker (tasks)

Can you think of colleagues who are 'all about the deadline'? They talk about 'milestones', 'goalposts' and 'getting things done'; they are driven by the practical process of achieving a result efficiently and effectively. People (themselves and others) are relevant in that they are resourced with skills that may be needed to accomplish the tasks, but people's feelings don't tend to feature in their conversations. These pragmatic thinking people are placing more focus on the extrinsic dimension and the task.

## The conceptual thinker (systems)

Do you find some people frustratingly insistent on understanding the 'why'? Why are we doing this? How does it fit with the visions, mission and purpose? How does this fit with the strategy? How does it comply with our principles and rules? These are the conceptual thinkers, for whom it is all about grasping the idea of the thing – its system. They are often black and white thinkers and tend to need a structure in place.

We each think in all three value dimensions but with different levels of focus and clarity. The overall combination of all employees' thinking styles represents the thinking talent of an organisation, and this underpins its culture. As humans are living and breathing beings (Maslow), subject to all manner of influences, so too is an organisation's culture. Our ability to make 'good' decisions and perform well at a particular time can go up as much as it can go down, based on personal circumstances and environmental factors; you will know this from your own experience. There will be some situations or cultures where you feel more comfortable and some settings and scenarios where you feel 'on fire', able to make significant decisions and get great results consistently. You will also have other examples of experiences where the culture, team or situation didn't work for you and this hampered your ability to make decisions and perform. While we may not always be able to change this, we can come to understand and even predict this, working to put ourselves in situations and cultures which are most likely to work well for us.

## What is Axiometrics®?

We opened this chapter with an explanation of Axiology, the philosophical study of value and have looked at ways to use this to determine how an individual values the world and themselves, and to explore how they think and make decisions. We now move to consider how this can be used to more accurately predict future behaviour, taking into account 'real life' variables and the specific capabilities of that individual.

This extension to standard Axiology is known as Axiometrics®, and it was developed by Dr Wayne Carpenter, a student of Hartman at the University of Tennessee and later chair of Axiometrics International (A*i*).[49] Dr KT Connor describes Carpenter's contribution to developing further Hartman's formal theory: 'The student, Wayne Carpenter, was to take that theory and refine its measurement, producing instruments that have been used over the past 30 years to measure, objectively and specifically, people's thinking and deciding capacities.'[50]

While stationed at Fort Benning during the Vietnam War, Carpenter was commissioned to develop a command decision manual for decision-making simulation exercises in helicopters. While researching the various decision theories proposed over the centuries to explain what influences an individual's actions, Carpenter realised that Hartman's Formal Axiology was a direct continuation of this field of study. What he had previously seen as the exciting explorations of one of his professors took on new weight and possibilities and, excited by the applicability of what Hartman had theorised, Carpenter decided then to devote his life to working with Hartman and his theory.

This partnership was not to last long, however, coming to an abrupt end with Hartman's untimely death in 1973. Hartman's widow gave Carpenter her husband's profile interpretation notes, and in his work since, Carpenter's focus has been on developing, validating and extending Hartman's work. This was the beginning of the steady process of building a solid system of axiological measurement that continues to this day.

The result of Carpenter's work is the development of a measurement system that captures an individual's unique thinking patterns and decision-making processes to a degree not possible with conventional self-report assessments.

'From his patented Axiometrics® system, Carpenter has produced analyses of thinking and decision-making competencies that focus not only on *how* people think and value but also consider *what* they value. The system also takes into account the organisational context they are operating in and how that might be impacting their ability to perform both in the present and the future. It is both of these, and especially the latter, that has provided the rich resource for the subject of this paper, the analysis of ethical alignment.'[51]

---

 If you would like to watch a short video overview of the applications for Axiometrics®, scan the QR code or follow this link: *www.catapult-solutions.co.uk/about/how-we-work/one-tool-multiple-applications-maximum-roi*

---

## Why conventional methods fail

It is almost universally the case that, as people, we do not know ourselves well; this is especially true of cognitive traits: few people give a lot of consideration to how they think. As individuals, there is a lot of pressure to present an overwhelmingly positive picture of oneself, especially in hiring/promotion situations. To counter this, many assessments include a 'fake good' scale which tries to detect people who are lying about themselves.[52]

Behavioural and personality assessments generated through inductive reasoning and self-reporting tend to assume that individuals will make the 'right' decisions when deciding what behaviour is needed to generate the best result. Psychometric tests are instead based on the interpretation of observed behaviour; trends and patterns within the observed group are then interpreted to create a 'norm', an understanding of how these are distributed through this reference population. However, it is important to understand that these norms will vary across different population groups (affected by factors such as culture, age, sex, and so on), making a direct comparison of like with like impossible.

As an organisation working in a virtual environment, you are focused on creating innovations that will take your business to the next level. This could be considering elements such as how to serve your clients more effectively; how to be more financially stable; or how to operate within an increasing number of compliance frameworks and yet remain agile as a business, for example. Whichever the current drivers for your business, you will generate the best solutions when you have input and ideas from a wide range of different perspectives; your ability to innovate is dependent on what we like to call your 'thinking diversity'.

Conventional assessment tools are limited to giving you information about an individual's view of their own personality or preferred behavioural style. Although useful to some degree for assessing self-awareness, this highly subjective information is not helpful when creating virtual teams which, by their nature, require their team members to work remotely and alone. This requires absolute certainty about the competency and confidence of the individuals within the team to make consistently 'good' decisions and act upon them. The ability to trust individuals to 'do the right thing' – especially when supervision may not be practicable for extended periods – is critical for credibility and vital for reputation.

Formal Axiology does not have these failings. It is a deductive social science. Deductive sciences begin with theories and move to specific, measurable applications and predictions. The job of the scientist in a deductive science is to test the theories against measurable reality. Physicists, mathematicians, doctors, statisticians and engineers are always comparing the implications and applications of their theories to reality. Formal Axiologists do the same. All other branches of the social sciences (philosophy, psychology, anthropology, sociology, etc) are inductive. Inductive sciences begin with specifics gained through observation, move to general conclusions that are based on observations of populations or groups, and then move back to specifics. Inductive reasoning relies on patterns and trends, while deductive reasoning relies on facts and rules.

More than ever before, the Three Dimensions of Value are now a real consideration in business and governmental decisions. As technology advances and the global economy continues to integrate cultures and merge ideas, organisations require unprecedented flexibility and the capacity to adapt quickly to change. These attributes are directly related to the value of talent and decision-making capabilities among the organisation's individuals.

It is likely that at some point in your career you have taken some sort of personality or behaviour questionnaire which will have given you a label (eg introvert/extrovert,

Myers-Briggs personality type, plant/completer/finisher), and with that, there will be associated expectations. What self-reporting tools cannot tell you is how accurate is your personal view of who you think you are or how you are likely to behave in any given situation. These tests are not objective and this makes direct comparisons between individuals impossible. To quantify and compare, we need to generate fixed points against which we can chart our results. However, as is often the case with psychological concepts and variables, trying to apply these scientific principles to the results from personality tests has severe limitations. As articulated by Paul Kline:

'There are no units of [psychological] measurement and no true zeros. …If we consider what is meant by intelligence or extraversion, just, for example, it is by no means clear what units of measurement might be used or what the true zero may mean.'[53]

There are also further limitations, as these tests were not designed with assessing suitability and capacity for working virtually in mind. To assess this would require slightly different types of questions – ones that are likely to make it even harder for the candidate to be wholly honest, when answering how they see the current/future 'real' them. They would need to explore issues around self-esteem, role-awareness and self-direction to identify how these enable or prevent an individual's view of themselves from becoming a reality. However, these are also the areas most likely to reveal our true vulnerabilities, ie the intangible factors or hidden variables that prevent us become our ideal version of ourselves.

Let's think about this logically. If you were asked any of the following questions in an interview for a new job or a promotional situation, how would you *honestly* answer?

- Do you value your self-worth?
- Do you have all of the competencies needed for this multifaceted role?
- Do you believe that this promotion will help you achieve your goals?

How can an individual ever provide a totally reliable and replicable assessment of who they are? To do this, there would need to be universally accepted and agreed standards for specific personality traits against which an individual could measure themselves, but even then, the results obtained through self-assessment would be highly subjective. If there are no true zeros in psychology, nothing can be objectively quantified or qualified. These limitations prove hugely problematic when trying to accurately understand a culture, generated as it is from a collection of individuals, and then to assess whether an individual can perform in the virtual culture you are looking to create. When assessing suitability for working in a virtual environment, where individuals can be given far more autonomy and make decisions for themselves, we need to look far deeper than simply understanding the personality or behavioural preferences of that individual, and also consider them in the context of their environment and the existing team. It is not enough to look at the individual in isolation from the culture.

## Creating a good culture

To create a good culture, we first require a robust methodology to define it, and then an understanding of how each team member can 'access their talent' and perform in that environment. To understand how you should build a good culture, you need to answer two overarching questions:

1. What does 'good' look like for us as an organisation?

   Answer this by considering:

   - The reason for the organisation: What are we here for?

   - How do we achieve this?

   - Who do we need to be to do this?

2. What culture do we need to create so that our leaders and employees can deliver 'good'?

   Answer this by considering:

   - What are the rules that we need?

   - What are the processes (including technology) that we need?

   - How do we treat and value our people to enable them to perform fully and consistently deliver 'good'?

Just as you have your individual leadership style, your organisation will also have its own unique culture which can positively or negatively affect the ability of you and your team members to 'access talent' and perform at their best.

## Hartman's 9 Performance Pathways

Hartman gave us a way to define a 'good' culture based on 9 Performance Pathways that can be used to assess the basic needs that underpin all groups.

1. **Building trust and the common bond:** As a baseline, this essential element requires that you see each person as unique, valuable and deserving of your respect.

2. **Building team synergy:** Synergy is when two or more discrete influences or agents acting together create an effect greater than that predicted by the effects of the individual agents when acting alone.

3. **Setting vision, mission and purpose:** One of our greatest needs is to have a sense of purpose and to be part of something other than ourselves.

4. **Instilling responsibility and integrity:** Leaders must create an environment where people feel responsible and accountable for their choices, with a clear understanding of their roles, expectations and how to meet them.

5. **Getting results:** This is about focusing on results and outcomes first, then moving to identify innovative ways to accomplish them.

6. **Developing strategies and discipline:** This is the personal discipline of identifying potential obstacles and developing strategies for overcoming them. It is the ability to predict, track and measure the relative success of decisions.

7. **Fostering innovation and change:** This is about creating a culture that encourages, supports and rewards innovation and change. It requires an adaptive growth model that facilitates trial, embraces error and encourages learning.

8. **Preparation and tactics:** This is about personal competence and confidence in decision making. It is directly affected by the ability of both the individual and company to accept and deal with problems, generating positive solutions.

9. **Maintaining consistency and conformity:** This is a respect for authority, rules, codes and property. There is an emphasis on and a willingness to meet established standards. This is setting goals that are challenging but attainable, both short and long term.

Having a clear understanding of these nine pathways and what it means to you and your team will help you build a good culture for your organisation.

# Two Worlds and Three Dimensions

We have already studied how Hartman developed his value science by applying his three value dimensions (intrinsic, extrinsic and systemic). When creating a tool to understand and report on human thinking and evaluating, Hartman realised that we apply these three dimensions to two different thinking processes. Return to the illustration once again and you will notice two boxes ('world' and 'self') associated with each of the three dimensions:

1. **The World:** How we view and perceive the environment outside of ourselves

2. **The Self:** How we view and perceive our inner selves and everything relating to our inner thinking

Each pathway has a particular alignment to one of the values for each of the two views, the world-view and the self-view, as illustrated in this table.

The world-view is the 'value talent' and the self-view is the 'talent enabler'. People may have talent, but they do not always have access to their talent. For example, 'self-limiting beliefs' hold people back from realising their potential. The good news is that our ability to develop clarity and focus in each of the three dimensions of both our world-view and self-view can be modified and changed, as we shall see.

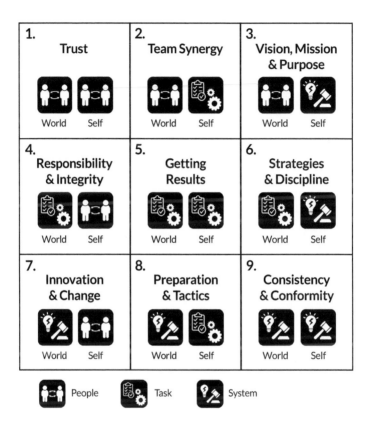

## Summary

In this chapter, we have introduced some key concepts that we will return to again and again throughout the book. The work of Maslow and Hartman underpins this book and offers a framework to inform your work to develop your workplace culture. The following chapters will explore each of the nine pathways in turn. We will also introduce several tools and techniques to help you lead better and build a robust and healthy culture in our VUCA world.

# SECTION TWO
## THE HOW

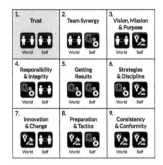

# 3

# Pathway 1: Building Trust And The Common Bond

## Trust defined

**To build trust within a group, you must view each person as unique, valuable and deserving of your respect.**

It is challenging to define trust, yet we instinctively know when it's gone; when trust is lost, we withdraw our energy and engagement. We can lose trust in a split second. Confidence evaporates when we fail to meet expectations. Trust is also contextual. To explore trust, we must first ask ourselves, 'What is it that I am trusting them to do, and why?'

Accepted wisdom decrees that trust builds over time and is therefore characteristic of long-term relationships; in the world of business, we need to find ways to expedite this process. Trust-building is a particular challenge for virtual teams where face-to-face contact is limited, or in hybrid models where there's a split between office-based and home-based colleagues, and the benefits that arise from social bonding are harder to facilitate in each case.

## Why is Trust the first of the nine pathways?

Trust is the currency of all good teams and organisations. It is essential for positive working relationships because it is central to engagement, and it fosters a willingness to co-operate and collaborate. When trust is present, we willingly commit our dedication, talent and energy and feel confident enough to share our honest thoughts and ideas. By contrast, teams dissolve and dissipate when there is no trust. Trust becomes even more critical during periods of change and volatility. People experience trust in different ways, which we explain later in this chapter. Individuals feel it in their gut (intuitive thinking); some develop it through actions (pragmatic thinking), and some place trust in titles and structure (systemic thinking). At least two parties are required to build trust – one receives it and one delivers it. It's an equation. People experience trust in different ways, and this is why it is so difficult to establish. This individual preference to place different emphasis on each of the three dimensions applies to all of the nine pathways. Therefore, it is imperative to use the same value framework to define the culture you are looking to create and then measure that talent against the same framework to inform development needs and enable vision alignment.

The study of trust encompasses concepts as diverse as ethics, morals, emotions and values, and academics have twisted themselves in knots attempting to decode the intractable concept of trust. Thankfully, Hartman's bold theory cut the Gordian knot,[54] demonstrating that there are only three fundamental ways in which trust is built and that that is via the three value dimensions.

# How to build the Trust Pathway

## The Trust Pathway in the three value dimensions

You can build trust by considering the three value dimensions:

1. **People** (intrinsic), 'intuitive thinking': Treating each person as unique and valuable.

2. **Task** (extrinsic), 'pragmatic thinking': Building confidence and competence.

3. **System** (systemic), 'systemic thinking': Respecting the rights of each person.

This table is a summary of the main axiological trust statements; the complete list runs to twelve strengths and twelve toxic factors.

|        | Strengths | Toxicities |
|--------|-----------|------------|
| *People* | Must develop and maintain trust from others | Will not be concerned by the needs or issues of others |
| *Task* | Must motivate others in a positive and reinforcing way | Will not take the time to make others feel worthwhile |
| *System* | Must be open to listening to others' views without personal bias | Will advise others in a superior, critical way |

Let us consider each of these dimensions of value in turn.

## People: Building trust by treating each person as an individual

Let's illustrate this with an example. On an average day, around lunchtime, Executive Chairman of Marriott International, Bill Marriott, would regularly visit the staff cafeteria on the ground floor of the Marriott Hotels headquarters. He'd pick up a tray, choose some food, stand in the queue and pay for his meal just like any other employee. He'd then pick a table and enjoy his lunch with anyone who wished to join him.[55] Despite his status as executive chair and one of the wealthiest people in the country, Bill eschewed special treatment. He showed up for lunch as an ordinary person, just as he did for board meetings. He brought interest, presence and care rather than status, hierarchy and power when engaging with employees and clients. Intuitive value is something that we feel, and Bill Marriott created trust with his employees by making each one feel seen and valued as a unique and precious individual.

## When this trust fails

Time for a story from Richard's early corporate career, entitled 'The absence of personal trust'.

It was the year 2000. I had just been headhunted into an international oil company as a sales manager along with a few sales executives who also 'took the shilling'[56] on the back of their strong track record in the Fast Moving Consumer Goods (FMCG) sector. After a year, an attractive US-based role was offered to one of my close ex-FMCG colleagues by his boss. My colleague flew out to Texas to inspect some schools, view a selection of rental properties and generally consider life stateside. His boss extolled the virtues of this promising new life but HR and upper management were not aware of this rosy propositioning. This situation felt wrong but I had no evidence to validate my concerns. My gut screamed that this executive was only promising this US-based role as a fabricated carrot to compel my colleague to work impossible hours and make unrealistic delivery commitments, which would also implicate my team. I tried to break the spell: 'He is selling you a pipedream; this will come to nothing.' My colleague was utterly gung-ho by this point and spent a lot of time travelling and socialising with his boss. He refused to listen to my repeated concerns, but sure enough, after six months of exhausting hours and empty promises, the new role came to nothing. My colleague and his family were crestfallen and hugely disappointed; he left the company within six months.

Trust can be difficult to pin down but place your trust in an untrustworthy person and odds are that you will get burned. If you ever start to feel uneasy, listen to these gut feelings, and ask a savvy, trustworthy colleague that you can trust to give you their honest and unvarnished view on the situation.

## Task: Building trust by building confidence and competence

Confidence and competence are observable. Competence in an individual will build confidence, provided that the organisational environment is conducive for the individual to give of their best.

Again, Richard will share a personal example.

I have a friend called David, who has built up a successful leisure and indoor climbing business in my local city, Leeds, in the north of England. Among his employees, David had identified a junior hourly-paid worker who showed great promise and had a genuine passion and talent for customer service. David was keen to build the talent of this young starter for eventual promotion to a senior management role, so he arranged an apprenticeship and internal training to provide her with the necessary management skills. He praised her generously, and as she developed her skills in her new role, she became increasingly confident and was, in turn, supported to take on more responsibility. David created a work environment that valued learning and encouraged progression across the team; competence building led to growth in confidence, and a growing sense of satisfaction and fulfilment among the young starter and those around her. By providing this practical worked-based education, support and training programme, David built a high system-based trust within the organisation.

### *When this trust fails*

We place a lot of faith in technology. When it fails, that is considered task-based failure. One striking example is the Windows phone. Microsoft dominated the business computing world with its ubiquitous PCs and Windows technology. When they launched the Windows phone in 2010,[57] it would have been reasonable to expect that the technology giant and its software would be successful in the mobile world.

And yet, Microsoft withdrew its Windows phone from all markets in 2017. One of the reasons was that the technology was simply not good enough. Today's digital-savvy consumers like to use a wide range of apps on their smartphone. The Windows phone did not have enough apps. In technical language, there was 'a lack of an application ecosystem – even as the company worked to encourage app developers and even wrote its own software'.[58]

## System: Building trust by listening to others' views without personal bias

Each of us is unique. As a result, we look at the world in different ways. We may encounter the same scenario as others but we will each view the experience through our own lens, noting different aspects, causes, interpretations and solutions for the same event. A lack of appreciation of this inherent individual bias is too often one of the root causes as to why some people find it difficult to get along. Despite efforts to avoid and eliminate it, we are all subject to unconscious bias. We each have a personal world-view and interpretation of the system, ie how we believe things ought to be, and we can often become dogmatic about right and wrong. This is a thinking bias.

To lead successfully, leaders need to understand and accept these inevitable thinking biases, recognising them in themselves as much as in others. Be aware that our individual bias will be heavily influenced by internal and external factors, such as gender, ethnicity, age, disability and sexual orientation. Valuable variation in thought, belief and approach needs to be included and embraced. Studies have found, and been concurred by the Equal Employment Opportunities Commission (EEOC), that Axiometrics® validates that there is insignificant difference in the thought structure that people use when they make decisions – between gender, age and creed categories.[59] As individuals, we all think differently, but there is not a different thinking type by category. In other words, not all women are gentle and nurturing – defined by their gender. The notion that the way to get diversity is to pick a selection of people from different groups is false. It's about the thinking diversity behind the eye. Teams with cognitive diversity can bring a range of diverse viewpoints to the table, and this can be invaluable when solving problems or innovating in the workplace. In other words, great minds think differently.

Can you remember an occasion when you put forward a good suggestion that was wholeheartedly ignored simply because it was something different from the generally perceived wisdom in the room? Conversely, can you think of leaders or colleagues who welcome innovative suggestions and ideas? Who actively listens, and asks questions to probe, explore and consider new recommendations or proposals? Which approach is most likely to build trust?

### When this trust fails

Systemic trust is when people trust somebody because of an existing system, eg their position. For example, many people have an inherent respect for and trust of doctors simply because of the position they hold within society. You may never have met them before, but because of their title, their white coat or the surgery or hospital desk, you automatically trust them. Just occasionally, but always tragically, callous individuals then take advantage of this systemic trust.

Dr Harold Shipman was an English general practitioner (GP) and 'believed to be one of the most prolific serial killers in modern history'.[60] In 2000, he was found guilty of murdering fifteen patients; but an inquiry later concluded that the total number of victims is likely to be about 250. He was able to commit multiple murders because his victims – mainly elderly women – trusted him, and as a result, he was able to exploit and then abuse the systemic trust that existed towards the medical profession in British society at the time.

# Who do you need to be to build Trust?

To build trust, you must first increase your self-awareness: How do you think, make decisions and view yourself and the world? How does your thinking pattern affect the way you build trust? These are big considerations and the answers lie beyond the scope of this book, but we can equip you with some questions and tools that will provide helpful indications of your thinking preferences. Bear in mind that this is a self-assessment exercise so your answers will be inherently subjective and unavoidably influenced by your own unconscious bias, as we have discussed.

To begin this exploration, let us consider each of the thinking tendencies in turn by asking yourself the following series of questions.

## Investigating your intrinsic thinking tendencies

- Has experience taught you that your gut instincts about people are usually right?

- Can you instantly tell if a friend or colleague is feeling 'out of sorts' just by looking at them?

- Do your initial feelings or first impressions about a person often prove accurate?

- Do you struggle to make a decision that you know will hurt someone?

- Do you feel it deeply when you are criticised by others? Do you find receiving criticism so painful that you experience it almost like a physical injury?

- Do you find that people tend to confide in you or turn to you to share their problems or concerns?

- At work, do you find that you tend to give poor performers multiple opportunities to improve when you should have acted sooner?

- Do you find yourself helping colleagues so much that you end up falling behind on your work?

## Investigating your extrinsic thinking tendencies

- Are you considered to be a practical problem solver?

- Do you find it easy to take a challenge and break it down into bite-sized tasks to formulate a plan to solve it?

- Do you have a reputation for getting things done on time and rarely miss a deadline?

- Do you tend to be on top of what is happening, able to form good assessments of progress, and know when to act when required?

- Do you tend to be critical and sometimes act too fast?

## Investigating your systemic thinking tendencies

- Do you believe that rules are sacred?

- Do you have to understand the 'why' before getting involved in a project?

- Do you feel uncomfortable if your expected standards are not being adhered to?

- Do you feel compelled to have a complete plan in place before beginning?

- Are you known for having excellent analytical abilities?

- Do you tend to see how things relate to one another in an orderly way?

- Do you find that you have a tendency towards a black and white way of viewing things and don't believe in 'grey areas'?

# Tools to help you build Trust

---

### TOOL: CONSIDERATIONS FOR REFLECTION – BUILD TRUST ON THREE LEVELS

Individuals: Leaders (and their team members) need to understand and trust their own judgement in a changing environment and have the self-belief and confidence to decide and take action.

Teams: Leaders need to understand the thinking and decision-making talent (which enables selection of the 'right' behaviour) of their team so that they can trust and therefore empower their team members. This means that individuals feel empowered, will increase their contribution and thus their unique talent is utilised.

Organisations: Leaders need the 'right' processes, communications, structures and rules in place that enable rather than hinder effective and efficient decision making.

---

## TOOL: PERSONAL SWOT ANALYSIS

Conduct a personal SWOT analysis, considering your strengths, weaknesses, opportunities and threats in turn, and ask others to provide input.[61] It is often most successful to do this via a 'Stop, Start and Continue' feedback structure as this conversational framework encourages people to both give and receive feedback openly and without fear of judgement or recrimination.

- Start by drawing up a SWOT analysis template, with one quadrant for each of the four SWOT factors. Divide each quadrant into three columns: People, Task and System.

| STRENGTHS | | | WEAKNESSES | | |
|---|---|---|---|---|---|
| People | Task | System | People | Task | System |
| **OPPORTUNITIES** | | | **THREATS** | | |
| People | Task | System | People | Task | System |

*Internal* (row label for STRENGTHS/WEAKNESSES)
*External* (row label for OPPORTUNITIES/THREATS)

- Ask colleagues or team members to tell you what they would like you to *stop* doing, *start* doing and *continue* doing; in return, you do the same for them.

- As you receive the feedback, transfer it onto your SWOT analysis template. For each comment, decide first where to place it within the S/W/O/T quadrants, and then in which of the three columns within that.

Once you have finished, look at your completed analysis tool and consider the results. How does this feedback compare with your answers to the self-assessment questions listed above? Are you surprised by the answers and how well people do or don't know you?

Remember not to take the results from this exercise too seriously. 360-degree feedback tools like this have spawned a whole industry, but as with any tool that relies on subjective human assessment, they are also inherently unreliable and changeable. Just as your self-assessment was affected by your own internal bias, so other people will have an inherent bias which will affect their ability to gauge objectively. The quality of the feedback will also be influenced by the widely differing motivations and concerns of individuals when providing feedback on their colleagues; this all assumes that they are clear and perceptive thinkers in the first place. These tools can provide useful information, but big career-progression decisions about potential suitability for roles and promotions should not be based purely on the analytic feedback tools–the broader picture also needs to be considered.

---

## TOOL: REFLECT ON YOUR IMPACT

Consider your experience of conflict in the workplace.

- Can you think of a time when you were shocked by the reaction of others to something you said, proposed or did?
- What was your intention?
- What was their perception of what you said or did?

We each have unique perspectives and world-views. Take time to reflect on your motivations and reasons on this occasion, and consider them within Hartman's three dimensions: intrinsic (people), extrinsic (task), systemic (system).

---

## TOOL: ASK FOR FEEDBACK

When you ask for feedback, this gives you a chance to consider the impact of your thinking style from the perspective of others. What's more, it can help you identify differences in how they think versus how you think, which can lead to a much better understanding.

---

# Pragmatic action list for building trust (people, task and system)

- **Don't ask a team member how they are – ask what you can do for them.** Acts of kindness can turn empathy into practical action and build trust.

- **Focus on integrity, not transparency (people).** Does copying your entire team in on every email serve to build trust? Before doing this, ask yourself, 'Do my motives for "copying all" align with the best interests of all parties? Am I including a wider audience purely to score points? Is my email unnecessary for many of these recipients?' Critically consider your logic and motivation. Are you guided by integrity or are you playing to the gallery?

- **Set clear expectations (system, task).** Be crystal clear about your expectations and desired outcomes when delegating tasks. Ask your team members to repeat back your request to ensure they have received and correctly understood your instructions. Once you have confirmed clarity, ask for their commitment to complete the task within a mutually agreed period.

- **Be consistent (system, task).** Publish a timetable for team meetings and stick to the schedule. Set recurring meetings for one-to-one meetings with team members. Predictability builds trust with systemic thinkers.

## Trust: Three questions

Take a minute to contemplate the following questions. Write down your answers. Then ask these same questions of your colleagues, peers and boss, about how they see you. Bear in mind that to answer they will reference their world-view and are likely to see things differently to you; do not be dismissive. There is only one response to give when receiving feedback: 'Thank you'; then move on, taking it on board to process later.

| People | Are you genuinely sensitive to your team's needs, concerns and perspectives? |
|--------|------------------------------------------------------------------------------|
| Task   | Do you feel that you receive suggestions from your team positively? |
| System | On projects, do you give the team the necessary confidence to take risks within the established boundaries? |

## Summary

Trust is the foundation of relationships, teams and organisational culture. We have explored how we build trust using the three dimensions: People, Task and System. We continuously use and blend these three, consciously or subconsciously, to build trust. In academic literature, trust is often seen as an elusive concept, difficult to define. That is because its formation is so situational, and the dynamics of the people involved inevitably mean that world-views and subconscious biases come into play and may even collide. Rather than seek to *define* trust, we suggest instead that you work to *design* trust using the three dimensions: people, task and system.

# 4

# Pathway 2: Building Team Synergy

## Team Synergy defined

Synergy occurs when team members start to work as one. They each contribute their diverse perspectives; assist one another to be more effective problem solvers; and recognise and affirm the contributions and success of each person to build strength, both individually and as a team.

The word 'synergy' comes (via Modern Latin) from the Ancient Greek word συνεργία (*synergia*), 'joint work, working together'. It combines two Greek words, *syn*, which means 'together' and *ergon*, 'work'. Simply put, synergy means 'working together'.[62]

Synergy is where two or more discrete agents act together to create a combined effect greater than the sum of the individual effects. While not strictly possible from a mathematical perspective, we can use a formula to illustrate the result that team synergy has on effect, where $2 + 2 > 4$.

## Why is Team Synergy the second of the nine pathways?

Trust is the foundation of a good team and organisational culture, and without it, team synergy is impossible. Trust leads naturally to a sense of belonging, loyalty to others and the team, and a sense of solidarity and shared purpose. When there is mutual trust, people feel free to be themselves and put forward their ideas or suggestions without fear of consequences or repercussions. Without this, innovation and progress will stall.

But trust alone is not enough. Good teamwork can achieve far greater results than the sum of the individuals working alone. Teams are better at innovation, idea generation and creativity than individuals. If you task one employee to solve a problem, how many different viable solutions could they produce? What if you then task multiple individuals to solve the same problem? What if, instead, you assign the problem to the entire team, but now working together? The team can now harness their collective power, identifying those with the highest skills in particular areas and allocating work accordingly, to best serve the collective purpose. How many more different and better solutions could they now generate, with each working to their strengths, but now amplified by the team synergy at play?

Teamwork improves productivity and brings better business results. Teams with high trust harness the thinking diversity of each person. With effective collaboration, you can get the best that everyone has to offer. The process of working together creates enthusiasm for idea generation, and sharing these ideas with a receptive team excites employees and accelerates the creative process. Team synergy will result in the generation of a bigger and better pool of ideas.

## How to build the Team Synergy Pathway

### The Team Synergy Pathway in the three value dimensions

Before you can begin attempting to build team synergy, you must have created a high-trust environment within your organisation.

There are a range of factors that fall into three areas which need to be focused on to build team synergy. For simplicity, we are using the three based on value dimensions: valuing people, putting in place short-term pragmatic action and developing longer-term plans and standards. For illustration, let's look at three examples with a primary grounding in each of the three dimensions.

|  | Strengths | Toxicities |
|---|---|---|
| *People* | Must set priorities in relationships with others | Will not pay attention to being fair and consistent |
| *Task* | Must be able to keep communications clear and to the point | Will not be willing to co-operate and share |
| System | Must be able to ensure that delegation of duties is assigned | Will not let others know what is expected of them |

## People: Building team synergy

In the 1930s, Walt Disney realised that he needed to hire more than 700 skilled artists and often travelled the country on recruitment road trips. Disney realised that building good working relationships with this community of artists would be the lifeblood of his company, so as an additional incentive, he offered to pay for schooling to improve their skills. In many black and white photographs from that era, Disney is often pictured around a drawing table or storyboard, meticulously plotting and crafting scenes and characters alongside the artists. A single story required thousands of hours of artistic input, and having effective and productive working relationships was essential. We are familiar with 'artistic differences' to explain why some creative projects fail; Disney found a successful way to generate positive relationships and shared priorities with the huge army of illustrators that he employed.

How did he achieve this success? One explanation is that he used a participative leadership style, which invites the opinions and ideas of all within the team before making a decision, enabling the leader to call on the combined expertise and talent of all team members.

This type of leadership is in stark contrast to the command-and-control style prevalent at that time, but Disney understood that he was not always the smartest in the room and there were people under him who could give valuable advice. Inviting all contributions enabled him to access the combined expertise and talent of all within the team.

## Task: Building team synergy

The team-building industry exists to organise activities and challenges to improve team communication and build team synergy. Richard shares a few examples from his corporate career to demonstrate how this can be done successfully.

> I remember organising a two-day event when I worked at Kellogg's. I called it the 'Keswick Challenge', and it took place in a historic Lake District hotel in Cumbria, in the north of England. The event centred around physical challenges, and we began by dividing people into pre-planned teams and gave each team long art straws. The challenge was simple: build the tallest stable tower using just the straws. The teams' collaboration initially suffered from scrambled communication, as the most vocal people talked over others and tried to impose their ideas. As the facilitator, I politely intervened and

suggested ways to enable all voices to be heard, and the teams gradually became more organised and agreed on ways to share and listen to ideas.

We then made indoor catapults from various pieces of wood and rubber bands. The objective was to fire a boiled egg as far as possible, and we used the hotel's grand ballroom. One team displayed excellent communication, clear talking and respectful listening. They built something that took us all by surprise, so powerful that they broke part of a glass chandelier with their catapult and egg!

I have undertaken similar team-building exercises all over the world. I have done raft building in early January in the Lake District and also in the Florida Keys – an experience a far cry from the freezing temperatures of the UK! I once ended up on the Great Wall of China, challenged to find and write down as many Chinese names as possible. I'll never forget a team go-karting race in Louisiana one night at a track next to a NASCAR track; the prize for the winning team was a hot lap on the track with a professional NASCAR driver. These events were all great fun, and there is no doubt that people who have shared these experiences form a strong bond while also learning practical lessons in keeping communications clear and to the point.

Top tip: The team leader should be heavily involved in designing the activities and facilitating them on the day to ensure that they are successful. Otherwise, if outsourced, a bond tends to form with the external organiser and becomes nothing more than a jolly on the company's expenses. Ownership, rather than outsourcing, taps into the people team synergy dimension and makes it more meaningful.

## System: Building team synergy

Leaders struggle to delegate if job descriptions and performance metrics are vague.

Clear job descriptions are an essential ingredient for team synergy. When colleagues are unclear on the scope of their role, their responsibility and accountabilities, how can they be measured or assessed? They will struggle with prioritisation and time management. How would they decide whether they could accommodate any additional requests from their boss if they are unclear of their existing workload and so cannot know if they have any capacity? Psychologists and economists will tell you this: humans modify their behaviour based on how they are assessed and rewarded. Anything you measure will drive a person to optimise their score on that metric. What you measure is what you'll get. Full stop.

Leaders will often claim that they are far too busy to delegate, that it's simply quicker and better for them to do it themselves. This excuse is a smokescreen. One of the most challenging transitions required for successful leadership is to move away from the 'doing' role. There's a psychological shift required to focus on more strategic areas and become less involved in the daily tasks. This brings us back to trust: leaders can't let go if they have not established sufficient trust within the team.

Delegation is something that many leaders find difficult. The answers lie in having a strong foundation of trust and the necessary systems to facilitate this. Leaders must put in place clear job descriptions and associated measurements, to support the expectation of their employees that they will be rightfully recompensed for accepting and completing delegated tasks.

# Who do you need to be to build Team Synergy?

## A cognitively-aware leader

Leaders must work on themselves before they can work on the team. This is not an act of selfishness. Think of it this way; in an airline safety briefing, you are told: 'In the unlikely event of an emergency, oxygen masks will appear from the overhead panel. Fit your own mask before helping others.' This goes against the instincts of many who would naturally help others before helping themselves, but if you think about it, the logic is sound: you must have a clear head to function well yourself before you can begin to help others. Our equivalent 'team synergy safety briefing' for leaders is this: 'If you experience business challenges, first understand how you make decisions – before you make decisions that will impact your team.'

This is *not* about emotional intelligence; it's deeper than that. It's about developing your cognitive intelligence by building your awareness and understanding of how you make decisions. Even the most successful professionals will occasionally face situations that challenge their strength and resilience, and they need to cultivate inner stamina to stay focused on directing their energy towards building team synergy. Developing this type of intelligence will improve your ability to handle these situations by taking a moment to check your thinking before acting in challenging situations. You can wreck a team in seconds via an outburst and decisions fuelled by emotion; it's far better to avoid that scenario.

## Aware of how you make decisions

Human nature means we view things through a personal lens and draw conclusions quickly. For example, when a person cuts you off mid-sentence, you may quickly conclude that 'they don't respect me.' We are quick to infer motives based on what we see, but this is problematic. Decision making based only on personal observations is akin to judging a book by its cover with no knowledge or consideration of the contents.

The trouble is, we're hard-wired to jump to conclusions; it's how our ancestors survived on the savannah when indecision over identifying a potential threat could cost your life. Our ancestral roots underpin many of our 'fight or flight' judgements, but this binary knee-jerk decision making is not always suited to our current environment. People still make these same 'friend or foe' decisions almost immediately, forming snap judgements on whether they like, trust or 'rate' a person, and these tend to become deeply entrenched.

Consider the words of an imaginary colleague: 'Oh, Julie is not going to like that; she always wants to have so much data and gather way too many views before she'll do anything.' From this, you infer that your colleague considers Julie a 'ditherer' and that her slowness in acting is because she is not as clever or as capable as those who make snap decisions and can talk confidently in meetings when justifying their view and actions to others. Later, you work alongside Julie on a project; her careful and methodical approach uncovers some surprising results and together you generate some innovative solutions to a long-standing issue within the team. Although reluctant to push herself forward, it is clear that Julie has real potential, her cautious exterior belying her sharp intellect and ability to see things from different and surprising perspectives. The first colleague had coloured your initial perceptions of Julie, and Julie quietly proved you both wrong.

This imaginary scenario is to demonstrate that it is dangerous to allow decision making, either by you or your colleagues, to be too heavily influenced by these snap judgements and assumptions. The opportunity to observe team members is reduced when there is reduced time shared on screen when you can only see each other in 2D observations are, by their nature, superficial. The etymology of the adjective 'superficial' is instructive. It comes from the Latin *superficiālis*, 'of or pertaining to the surface'. It is derived from *superficies* ('surface, upper side, top'), a combination of two Latin root words: *super* ('above, over'), and *facies* ('form, face').[63] Eliding these words gives us an elegant term that describes the notion of vision confined to the external surface.

Time to return from this linguistic foray. The point is this: you can't afford to be a superficial leader who is too heavily reliant on observation to inform your decisions. You need to look inside and question what is driving what you observe: why do people do what they do, and how do they make decisions? You need to become a cognitively-aware leader, but how can you develop this? In the next section, we provide tools to help increase your cognitive awareness which will help you build team synergy.

## Tools to help you build Team Synergy

If only we could trust everybody to do the right things in the right way all the time; people, teams and organisations would operate more efficiently and smoothly and we'd have fewer nasty surprises. Imagine being able to create a performance culture like this, despite having staff widely dispersed across work and home locations; how satisfying and productive that would be. Our first step toward building such a culture starts with exploring how we make decisions.

How often have you found yourself wondering, 'What were they thinking?' when faced with a colleague's unsound decision or problematic emotional outburst? Sometimes we end up asking the same of ourselves after we have made the wrong call or mishandled a situation. The keyword in all of this is 'thinking': too often, many of our daily decisions are made without thinking. As Charles Duhigg said in his book *The Power of Habit*, 'When a habit emerges, the brain stops fully participating in decision making.'[64]

But what is our actual thinking process when we make our decisions? Again, Formal Axiology has the answer.

## Five-step decision-making process

Hartman identified that there is a universal five-step decision-making process that takes us from cause to effect, from our values to our actions:

- When you **value** something, you refer to your existing experience and knowledge and therefore you are influenced by bias and prejudices.

- You then **evaluate** it via the three dimensions of value: intrinsic, extrinsic and systemic.

- When **thinking,** you consider each of the options available, before you then select one and make a decision.

- This decision is based on your **judgement** and evaluation of the scenario.

- **Action** then follows. This can be observed in your behaviour, reaction or even a decision not to act.

This diagram sets out the five steps in a pyramid. We recommend you read it from 'values' at the bottom to 'action' at the top. You'll notice a dotted line between 'thinking' and 'judgement'; this line is the decision line and indicates the point at which the decision is made. It also indicates the transition from sub/unconscious thinking to conscious thought. We can use Axiometrics® to clarify what is going on in the subconscious, where about 95% of our thinking takes place:[65] 'Figuratively speaking, it could be 99 percent; we probably will never know precisely how much is outside awareness.'[66]

When we assess a given scenario, we evaluate it against our intrinsic values or norms, and our environment hugely influences us. What we value is unique and shaped by various factors such as parents, friends, role models, education, local culture, media influences and so on. The list is endless, but despite this, Hartman found that we use the same three dimensions when we make our evaluations, regardless of the situation in question.

Now let's consider how this process affects our strengths and vulnerabilities as decision makers.

## Strengths as decision makers

- Our uniqueness as individuals (arguably our greatest strength, but also a weakness)
- Our ability to focus on a situation or problem
- Our ability to interpret what is happening
- Our ability to come to a decision
- Our ability to then translate the decision into action

# Five Step Decision Making Process

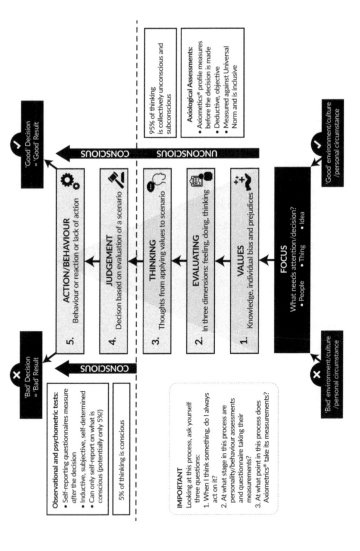

'Good' Decision = 'Good' Result

'Bad' Decision = 'Bad' Result

**CONSCIOUS**

**UNCONSCIOUS**

**CONSCIOUS**

95% of thinking is collectively unconscious and subconscious

**Axiological Assessments:**
- Axiometrics® profile measures before the decision is made
- Deductive, objective
- Measured against Universal Norm and is inclusive

'Good' environment/culture /personal circumstance

**5. ACTION/BEHAVIOUR**
Behaviour or reaction or lack of action

**4. JUDGEMENT**
Decision based on evaluation of a scenario

**3. THINKING**
Thoughts from applying values to scenario

**2. EVALUATING**
In three dimensions: feeling, doing, thinking

**1. VALUES**
Knowledge, individual bias and prejudices

**FOCUS**
What needs attention/decision?
- People  • Thing  • Idea

'Bad' environment/culture /personal circumstance

Observational and psychometric tests:
- Self-reporting questionnaires measure *after* the decision
- Inductive, subjective, self-determined
- Can only self-report on what is conscious (potentially only 5%!)

5% of thinking is conscious

**IMPORTANT**
Looking at this process, ask yourself three questions:
1. When I think something, do I always act on it?
2. At what stage in this process are personality/behaviour assessments and questionnaire taking their measurements?
3. At what point in this process does Axiometrics® take its measurements?

## Vulnerabilities as decision makers

- Our uniqueness as individuals

- Our limited ability to see the world from other perspectives, in different ways or using different tools

- Our tendency to pay attention selectively, focusing on some elements and leaving others out

- Our lack of understanding and appreciation of why others may see the same things differently

Hartman argues that, by using the same value framework to define 'good', we can come to better understand how an individual sees and values things, thereby gaining a better ability to predict their subsequent behaviour.

---

 If you would like to watch a video to learn more about effective decision making, scan the QR code of follow this link: *www.catapult-solutions.co.uk/about/how-we-work/effective-decision-making*

---

### TOOL: HOW TO APPLY THE FIVE-STEP DECISION-MAKING PROCESS

Remember that 95% of thinking is done in the subconscious and that we each have unique perspectives on a given situation. When we form an opinion on the action of another, it's the product of rapid hidden processing in our subconscious. However, we must also bear in mind that the person's action is being driven by thinking processes within their head, influenced by factors that you simply cannot know. In the absence of that knowledge, we tend to create our own narrative to explain what we have seen and why they did it. We all do this, it's called 'jumping to conclusions'.

Consider this illustration of how this can play out in the workplace:

- You are in a meeting room in which you are delivering a presentation to twelve people.

- You are surrounded by a lot of observable data and activity. Since you can't simultaneously take on board everything that is happening, you select what you can focus on. You notice that one of the twelve people is yawning and checking their phone.

- You don't know the true reason for this behaviour, so instead, you generate your own explanation, based on your own experiences, assumptions, beliefs and even stereotypes: 'That person is not paying attention to me.'

- You make assumptions about his apparent lack of attention: 'He is not interested in what I am saying.'

- This assumption then hardens within your mind as you extrapolate a possible explanation for this behaviour: 'He is competing with me and purposely trying to make me look stupid in front of our boss.'

Your conclusions have reinforced your anxieties and beliefs, and now influence how you then decide to act: 'I am going to make him look ignorant in front of our bosses in retaliation.'

Rather than jump to conclusions, why not test your assumptions formulated in the subconscious by asking questions; make the process of thinking through an explanation conscious and even collaborative. In the scenario above, consider asking, 'Has this presentation been useful to you?' You can even ask more direct questions designed to seek external explanations for what you have observed: 'You've been looking at your smartphone throughout the presentation; can I ask why?' To which the colleague might reply: 'Yes, this topic is so interesting! I've been checking my calendar to find when I can meet you to discuss it in more depth.' By checking your thinking, the outcome of this exchange could have been strikingly different.

---

### TOOL: CHALLENGE YOUR THINKING

Use your understanding of Hartman's five steps to help you draw better conclusions or challenge other people's findings based on a greater understanding of their decisions and behaviours.

Before acting, work through the following process:

1. Stop! Take time to consider your reasoning.
2. Ask yourself this series of questions to explore the process of making the decision:
    - Are you selecting your data or reality appropriately?
    - Are you interpreting what it means?
    - Are you making or testing assumptions?
    - Are you forming or testing your conclusions?
    - Are you now deciding what to do, and why?

3. Having made a decision, use these questions to test that decision:
   - Why have I made these assumptions?
   - Is this the 'right' conclusion?
   - Why do I think this is the 'right' thing to do?
   - Is this based on all the facts?
   - Why does s/he believe that?
4. Finally, consider the decision in the light of each of the three dimensions of value:
   - How do I feel about it?
   - What do I know about it?
   - What do I think about it?

---

## TOOL: DELEGATION AND COMMITMENT CONVERSATIONS

To harness team synergy, a leader must assign tasks clearly and precisely, and be confident that all duties have been appropriately delegated. Delegation is seen as an art but holding a 'commitment conversation' can make a successful outcome more likely. This is a framework that can be used to guide a conversation regarding the commitment of another to deliver on what is asked of them, to ensure absolute clarity about expectations on both sides.

To agree on a commitment to deliver, two components are required, both of which must be established with absolute clarity: the request and the response.

## 1. The request

A request for commitment needs to include four components:[67]

| | |
|---|---|
| Context on why this is important: | 'In order to achieve V, I need you to...' |
| Clarity on who is asking and who is being asked: | 'I request that you...' |
| Clarity on what is being asked and by when: | '... do W by X.' |
| A request for a commitment: | 'Can you commit to that?' |

If any of these elements are missing or unclear, you do not have a clear request.

## 2. The response

When you ask a request, you will receive one of two types of responses:

- Committed: There are only two possible committed responses to a request: 'Yes, I commit' or 'No, I cannot commit.'

- Uncommitted: There are, however, a large number of uncommitted responses that you could receive. Examples include: 'Leave it with me'; 'I will try my best'; 'Let me get back to you on that'; 'I can't promise, let's see how it goes.' If you accept unclear responses like these, it is hard to hold people to account for results. For example: 'I tried my best but I didn't succeed'; 'I didn't agree to that but I did what I promised I would, so why are you complaining?'

There may sometimes be a need for an intermediate step before the respondent can respond to the commitment response. Examples of such intermediate steps could include replies such as: 'Before I commit, I need clarification on...'; 'I commit to respond by date and time'; 'I decline but counteroffer to deliver Y by Z.'

### 3. Integrity in commitment conversations

Over time, you will build a reputation for your 'integrity in commitments', ie your reliability in delivering what you have agreed you will deliver. To consistently deliver on your commitments, you need to check that you can answer 'yes' to each of the following questions agreeing to the commitment:

- Do I understand what the other person is requesting of me?
- Do I have the skills and resources to do it?
- Am I convinced that those on whom I depend will deliver for me?
- Am I willing to be held accountable for nondelivery?

While these questions are for consideration by the performer, ie the person delivering the commitment, the customer (the person receiving delivery of a commitment) also has a responsibility to check that the commitment which they are demanding is realistic. If you know that someone is making an unrealistic commitment to you, having 'integrity in commitments' requires that you should raise your doubts.

---

### TOOL: FIVE QUESTIONS TO MANAGE INDIVIDUAL AND TEAM PERFORMANCE

Make a habit of regular check-ins with your colleagues. This can be face-to-face, by phone or virtual, and done on a one-to-one basis or as a team.

1. What have I/you/we achieved this week?
2. What's gone well?
3. What hasn't gone well?
4. What have I/you/we learned (people/task/system)?
5. What action do I/you/we need to take before our next check-in (people/task/system)?

## Team Synergy: Three questions

| | |
|---|---|
| *People* | Are you comfortable when listening to opposing points of view? |
| *Task* | Do you understand and value the diverse skills and talents of your colleagues? |
| *System* | Are you able to deal with conflicting issues in a positive manner? |

## Summary

The ability to infer correctly from conversations and situations is an essential cognitive skill. It helps us to interpret and give meaning to the world around us. We can best improve our communication and understanding by sharing our thinking processes, not only to explain the output but also to check in on and question our thinking. The key to building team synergy is to be a cognitively-aware leader and avoid jumping to conclusions, remembering always that cognitive diversity is your greatest asset.

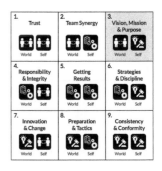

| 1. Trust | 2. Team Synergy | 3. Vision, Mission & Purpose |
|---|---|---|
| World Self | World Self | World Self |
| 4. Responsibility & Integrity | 5. Getting Results | 6. Strategies & Discipline |
| World Self | World Self | World Self |
| 7. Innovation & Change | 8. Preparation & Tactics | 9. Consistency & Conformity |
| World Self | World Self | World Self |

# 5
# Pathway 3: Setting Vision, Mission and Purpose

## Vision and Mission and Purpose defined

Let's start by distinguishing the terms. The concepts are often regarded as overlapping and used interchangeably. This is because an understanding of their true meaning is often not firmly established within the culture or operations of a business, and so people use the terms incorrectly or in an idiosyncratic manner. There is a distinct difference between' 'vision' and 'mission' and purpose and they are each rooted principally in one of the three value dimensions.

### Vision

The vision is about the future. A vision statement sets out the aspirations of the organisation and defines the direction, to generate a vision of the organisation in the future. Ideally, this vision is defined with representative involvement from all areas and levels of an organisation, to ensure it grows from within the organisation rather than being imposed upon it. The vision then provides the focus for your mission statement, setting out what the organisation needs to accomplish. Vision is rooted in systemic value. It's about setting out ideas, order, meaning, plans, goals, principles and standards for the future. The vision is the *what*, ie the picture of the future.

## Mission

The mission is about the everyday. The mission statement describes the business of the organisation and also lays out what it isn't. It sets out what your organisation does and for whom, thereby providing focus and establishing clear boundaries for management and staff. The mission is rooted in pragmatic value. It's about properties, parts, steps, tangible goals, processing the environment, the 'real world in real-time'. The mission is the *how* of the organisation.

## Purpose

As individuals, we have a core need to have a sense of belonging, to feel part of something larger than ourselves. In the last few years, there has been a lot of talk about the concept of purpose. Purpose is a by-product of a good culture. Maslow's idea of self-actualisation came from a humanistic perspective. Humanistic psychologists argue that people are driven by higher needs. However, when setting a Vision, Mission and Purpose, they need to be set in that order; in other words, head, hand, heart. The head sets out the vision for the future. The mission is the hand, setting the activities that need to be carried out to achieve the Vision. Only then can the purpose be set, since without the framework established by Vision and Mission, the heart has nothing to connect with. Once the Vision, Mission and Purpose have been set, it is time for delivery. This time the sequence is different, beginning with the heart, followed by the hand and then head. In other words, people need to first connect to the purpose with their heart on an intuitive level (intrinsic), which motivates them to do the doing (i.e. the hand – extrinsic), which is the practical way of delivering the vision (the head – systemic).

## Why is Setting Vision, Mission and Purpose the third of the nine pathways?

The mathematical and logical system of value concepts is the cornerstone of Hartman's Formal Axiology. Hartman discovered that all value has scientific order, based on transfinite mathematical sets, and a value hierarchy in the three dimensions of value. He identified the principles that order and structure our moral decisions and our value judgements.

It has been instructive to note the balance of these three values at play as the governments of the world responded to the COVID-19 pandemic; although their eventual solutions were slightly different, these decisions were all governed by the same principles as each government tried to balance their duty to take care of their people (intrinsic value) and introduce legal measures e.g. mask wearing, social distancing, vaccination (systemic value) and by putting in place pragmatic actions such as the furlough schemes (extrinsic value). The maths is complex, but the logic is clear. The highest mathematical value is intrinsic, the extrinsic value follows this, and finally, there's the systemic value. In real terms, this means that people should come first, then practical matters and finally, the plans and policies.

Although this hierarchy is well established, cultures can have an inherent bias when applying the value dimensions. Again, we saw this in the pandemic: New Zealand put people first; Brazil put the economy first; China was swift to put in place a set of rules. This also applies to organisational cultures. However, the nine steps to build a good culture are sequenced according to their relative mathematical value order.

Trust is wholly rooted in the intrinsic value dimension; Team Synergy is part intrinsic and part extrinsic – as we saw in the previous chapter, a leader needs to use some practical tools to help build and maintain team synergy through valuing the uniqueness of each individual. Vision, mission and purpose is part intrinsic and part systemic. They make purpose possible which appeal to people's humanity and heart, but they also involve looking into the future and establishing a path forward.

In recent years, there has been a lot of focus on organisations defining their vision, mission and purpose, as a primary step in leading an organisation, or as a necessary starting point for introducing a new strategy and direction. Some might argue that you need to get this vision stuff in place before you can work on building the culture, but we have already established that the order of the nine pathways is dictated by a mathematical hierarchy. The rationale is clear: if there is low trust, people will not feel comfortable sharing or contributing their ideas to the vision and mission. Also, not everybody can be involved in defining the vision, so people will have to trust senior management to facilitate the creation of the vision, mission and purpose. No matter how compelling the vision, mission and purpose are, people won't buy into it if they don't trust their senior leadership. If there is low or no team synergy, teams can't rally around a vision effectively. The vision statement becomes nothing more than something that adorns the office wall. Organisations often say that they put people first; this is easy to say but it's not so easy to deliver a culture that truly achieves this.

## How to build the Setting Vision, Mission and Purpose Pathway

### The Vision, Mission and Purpose Pathway in the three value dimensions

First, you need to have worked through the first two steps to create a high-trust environment and build team synergy. When it comes Pathway 3 and defining Good Vision,

Mission and Purpose note that this is the only pathway where we focus on the System first, followed by Task, followed by People. This is because we need to know where we are going, the resources that we will need and who we need to be as a group of people in order to achieve our purpose.

Once Vision, Mission and Purpose has been defined, we deliver this element of a Good Culture by focusing first on the people, valuing their uniqueness to align them to the Mission and Vision by establishing a personal connection to the journey and outcome.

The vision is based on longer-term plans and standards. The mission focuses on putting in place short-term pragmatic action steps.

For illustration, let's look at three examples:

|  | Strengths | Toxicities |
|---|---|---|
| People | Must reinforce a personal commitment to strive to do one's best | Will focus on their priorities at the expense of the team |
| Task | Must be able to communicate optimism, vision and purpose | Will have difficulty keeping their word and commitments |
| System | Must be able to maintain a strong sense of direction and purpose | Will not consistently push to achieve their goals |

## People: Building Personal Commitment and Purpose

An organisation creates a picture of its desired future when it defines its vision for the future, and it describes its mission which explains how the vision will be achieved. None of these exercises matter if leaders and employees don't have an intrinsic connection to the vision and mission. Therefore, it is important to demonstrate personal commitment to strive towards doing the best to achieve the vision and mission. This is how the personal connection is forged and becomes what is known as purpose.

## Task: Building mission

An excellent example of a vision-inspired mission statement is IKEA's: *'To create a better everyday life for the many people.'*[68] Their mission statement could have been about selling well-designed, affordable furniture, but instead, it goes beyond this to include a visionary element. IKEA's mission and business model are akin to a partnership with its customers: IKEA scours the world for deals and buys in bulk, then we choose the furniture and pick it up at a self-service warehouse for DIY assembly at home. IKEA's mission is to serve its customers and meet their needs in a way that is accessible and appealing, but it is also aspirational, promising its customers a 'better everyday life'. It certainly ticks the box for optimism!

## System: Building vision

Project your goals into the future. Imagine your organisation in five or ten years. Your vision statement should express the future that you have just envisioned. Remember that this is a vision and not a step-by-step implementation plan.

Use the following questions to help you clarify your vision:

- Where do we want the organisation to go?

- What can we realistically achieve?

- What problems is the organisation designed to solve?

- What changes do we believe the company can make for individuals? For the industry?

- How will things be different once the vision is realised?

# Who do you need to be to Set Vision Mission and Purpose?

To build the Setting, Vision, Mission and Purpose Pathway successfully, you need to have a solid understanding of the three dimensions of values. This will then enable you to make several practical changes to both your leadership style and the culture of the organisation. These include the following six steps.

## 1. Have the foundations in place

You must first have prioritised and become proficient at building trust and building team synergy. As outlined in the previous chapter, this requires you to develop your cognitive skills, understand how you make decisions, look for the differences and appreciate how the thinking of others is driving their decision making, actions and behaviour.

## 2. Be intentional when designing the vision, mission and purpose

You need to make intentional use of the three value dimensions to lead a collaborative effort to build the commitment (people), mission (task) and vision (system) for your organisation. Many companies don't distinguish between these values and this results in a blurred message that fails to engage their employees. Hartman deduced and then demonstrated that everyone makes decisions using the Three Dimensions of Value, ie that the structure of thought has this single norm. This Axiometrics® norm is inclusive: it has been proven by the Equal Employment Opportunities Commission (EEOC) to apply to people worldwide, regardless of culture, race, income, age, gender or other factors.[69] We all have the same structure of thought.

## 3. Communicate in three dimensions

When communicating to colleagues, staff and stakeholders, structure your messaging using the three value dimensions. In this way, you will appeal and connect with the audience since this structure of thought is common to all.

- **People:** What is in it for you? What are the benefits and implications for people? Consider and address the impact on all stakeholders.

- **Task:** Be clear on the steps and what you are communicating. What do people need to do now?

- **System:** How does your message connect with the strategy, previous plans, rules and regulations?

## 4. Listen for purpose

When people don't have a willing commitment to a purpose, you can hear it in their language. For example, you call Bob for a catch-up but he sounds flustered as he answers: 'Oh, I don't have time to chat! I have to get the sales forecast completed or else the boss will be furious, and you know what that's like!'

What's happening here? Notice the language: '*I have to… or else…*'; Bob is clearly afraid of negative consequences should he fail to deliver. This is a stress-generating cycle. As leaders, you need to be facilitators of commitment, not figures of fear. Connect people to a vision and mission and listen to how the language of purpose changes.

Let's re-enact the same scenario. You call Bob: 'Oh, hi! Let's have a quick catch-up chat.'

Bob replies: 'Sorry, I can't talk now. I want to get the sales forecast finished. Once my numbers are in, the supply team can organise the correct quantity and mix of products for my customers.'

In this version, Bob is committed to a mission. Notice the language, '*I want... because...*'. Bob now has a positive reason for not stopping to chat to you, and his decision is driven by desire and motivation, not by fear. He is acting on purpose.

When you hear people saying that they *want* or *choose* to complete tasks, rather than *having* to do things, this is indicative of their connection and commitment to the mission. People who understand the vision and feel connected to the mission are more likely to be energetic and positive. Increased job satisfaction boosts productivity. Listen out for negative language or signs of unhealthy motivations, and take them as a red flag for your culture. Ask questions of yourself. Do we need to do more work to build trust and team synergy? Are the, vision, mission and purpose not currently resonating with the workforce?

In the first chapter, we listed Hartman's four questions for reflection to help people align their personal purpose to the organisation

- What am I here for in the world?
- Why do I work for this organisation?
- What can this organisation do to help me fulfil my meaning in the world?

- How can I help this organisation help me fulfil my meaning in the world?[70]

Hartman's framework enables people to achieve Maslow's self actualisation.

## 5. Keep on track: Use the language of commitment

Check your words and listen to your language. As explained earlier, it's essential to use the language of choice: 'I want us to deliver because…'; I want us to look at this setback'; or 'Let's deal with reality, I want us to succeed.' Develop an awareness of the language of choice and learn to check and catch yourself if you find yourself slipping. It can be easy to slip into the language of compulsion: 'To avoid this problem… '; 'To make this deadline, we must do… '; or 'We have to…'. If you only paint a picture of obligation, failure, missing out, catastrophe, disaster and fear, this will generate stress and cause people to lose motivation and creativity. It's much better to be a mindful leader who leads with the language of choice.

There will, of course, always be occasions, events, triggers and people that can cause you to experience an immediate, strong, negative emotional reaction. This often happens when you face criticism. It's essential to listen to the other person openly and consider the situation as broadly as possible. Make it your mantra to take what they are saying and view it relative to the context of your purpose. Resist the urge to interrupt. Reflect and ask questions to clarify. Ask yourself, 'Is this situation, and my reaction to it, going to help or hinder our progress towards our team purpose?' Before answering, consider your language to make it clear that you are exercising choice connected to the vision or mission. Don't allow yourself to start indulging in blame and excuses; getting stuck in recrimination and condemnation is hardly likely to encourage your team's creativity, innovation and motivation.

As a leader of a team, you must demonstrate insight and that can only be achieved if you are clear-headed, calm and connected to the vision and mission. As a leader, you're a facilitator of engagement, and this means you must be engaged yourself. Leaders must 'walk the talk'. You must be relentless – almost obsessive – in repeatedly referencing and restating your objectives in relation to the vision and mission each time there's a new meeting and new initiative. Repeat, repeat, repeat! Always refer decisions, explanations and changes back to the organisation's vision and mission. This way, leaders can start to put in place structures, systems and cultural commitment to support the vision and mission, rather than just relying on effort or 'efforting', and work, work, work.

## 6. Maintain team Purpose by creating a heartbeat for your team

What does it take to get people engaged and committed? Well, it's not a one-time event; sure, invest in some grand future-gazing event where the team gathers for an awayday meeting or a virtual visioning session, but it's far better to put purpose into the team's 'heartbeat' – the ongoing pulse deep within that drives the organisation. For example, take the time to state the goal for every meeting or initiative. Say why you believe a particular course of action needs to happen and explain why you are launching a new initiative. Get that connection clearly articulated and allow people to ask questions and clarify it. It's an opportunity to reinforce the connection between the initiative and the vision, mission and purpose of the organisation.

Giving life and form to your team purpose will make you more resilient as a leader. When you are under pressure, such as, when launching an initiative against tight deadlines, you can end up becoming stressed and emotional when conveying the urgency of the initiative to your team. One way to control your response and manage unhelpful emotions is by connecting to your team and business vision and mission. It makes it easier to stay in control and calmly set out the scale of the challenge and the deadlines. Remember Hartman's four questions? If you understand people's purpose and what they hope to achieve in their careers, it helps you find their driving energy and connect that with the team purpose. You can't simply make people get motivated so instead, you must make a deeper connection to their purpose as individuals.

# Tools to help you Set Vision, Mission and Purpose

---

### TOOL: THE VISION ALIGNMENT MODEL

Establishing alignment of vision between individuals can be a problem. This diagram helps you draw together the essential elements as a leader. It shows how values can determine actions, and it can be used to check alignment (or its absence). Think of it as a navigation tool.

Let's start at the top. The globe represents the environment – the culture – in which we work. In the introduction we noted that culture can be summarised as 'the way things get done round here', and it is made up of the Vision, Goals and Strategies, and Values, that guide direction.[71] These elements are all needed for action to occur and for Culture to be considered synonymous with Cause. Above the line are attributes and components which are the causes/enablers of everything below line. Below the horizontal dividing line, four factors – Actions/Tasks, Systems and Processes, Skills, and Behaviours – 'effect' the Outcomes.

The major movement is from Vision at the top to Outcomes at the bottom, but the diagram is also divided in the vertical plane, linking *What we do* – Goals and Strategies, Actions/ Tasks, and Systems and Processes (on the left) – with *How we do it* – Values, Skills, and Behaviours (on the right), supported by the 9 Performance Pathways which, in turn, enable Culture, creating a virtuous cycle.

Two sets of contributory drivers provide further stimulus:

1. Access to Talent, and Attitude – these are enabled by, as well as influence, Culture

2. Talent and Skill – outside Culture at the level of the individual; these feed into Behaviours

These four drivers are defined below.

- Access to talent: Measures how well an individual can access their talent in a specific environment; 'access' is identified through a decision-to-performance ratio that considers specific capabilities associated with success on the one hand and distinct blocks that increase the risk of failure on the other.

- Attitude: A measure of bias in one's thinking that can enhance or hinder the ability to make accurate and reliable decisions. These biases result from too much or too little focus on certain factors in the decision environment.

- Skills: A performance ratio identifies and measures competencies that discriminate between high and low performance. Competencies are the result of the translation of decision talent into action.

- Talent: Talent is a measure of performance potential indicating how well an individual can maximise their strengths and minimise the impact of their weaknesses. It measures how well an individual thinks and makes decisions, what they pay attention to, and how well they perform specific decision tasks.[72]

Let's expand on this. Imagine working for a company with a culture that you don't subscribe to and find aggravating; would you be able to perform at your best? We are a product of our environment and it has a significant impact on how we act. People may thrive in one culture, but move to another company and find it hard to make headway. The critical point is that a difficult culture can hamper our ability to access our skills and talents. People who are successful within

# Vision Alignment Model

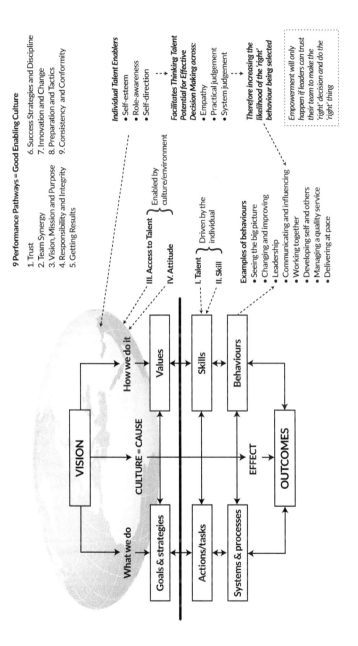

**9 Performance Pathways = Good Enabling Culture**

1. Trust
2. Team Synergy
3. Vision, Mission and Purpose
4. Responsibility and Integrity
5. Getting Results
6. Success Strategies and Discipline
7. Innovation and Change
8. Preparation and Tactics
9. Consistency and Conformity

*Individual Talent Enablers*
- Self-esteem
- Role-awareness
- Self-direction

***Facilitates Thinking Talent
Potential for Effective
Decision Making across:***
- Empathy
- Practical judgement
- System judgement

***Therefore increasing the
likelihood of the 'right'
behaviour being selected***

*Empowerment will only
happen if leaders can trust
their team to make the
'right' decision and do the
'right' thing*

III. Access to Talent } Enabled by culture/environment

IV. Attitude

I. Talent } Driven by the individual

II. Skill

**Examples of behaviours**
- Seeing the big picture
- Changing and improving
- Leadership
- Communicating and influencing
- Working together
- Developing self and others
- Managing a quality service
- Delivering at pace

VISION

CULTURE = CAUSE

How we do it

What we do

Values

Skills

Behaviours

Goals & strategies

Actions/tasks

Systems & processes

EFFECT

OUTCOMES

that difficult environment may have to adapt and modify the values, a process that then feeds back into driving that culture, so it can be hard to bring about any change.

The quality of Culture enables either Good or Bad Outcomes, as shown in the Consequences of a Good or Bad Culture diagram. The effects of a good culture (at the top of the diagram) together help to achieve strategic objectives; the effects of a bad culture (at the bottom) prevent it. This affirms the adage that 'Culture eats strategy for breakfast'.[73]

## TOOL: PERSONAL LEADERSHIP PURPOSE

Dig into your past to explore experiences that draw out common threads and significant themes, and you will soon begin to identify the things that energise you and bring you happiness. These are your inner core, your lifelong strengths, your values and your passions.

Ask yourself these five questions:

1.  What did you enjoy doing when you were a child before the world told you what you should or shouldn't like or do? Think of a specific occasion and how it made you feel.
2.  Describe two of your most challenging experiences. How have they shaped you?
3.  What activities make you lose track of time?
4.  What kinds of issues do people ask you to help with?
5.  What do you most enjoy doing?

Tackle these questions in a small group of colleagues or friends. You can't get a clear picture of yourself without the added input and perspectives of people you trust.

After this reflective work, take a shot at crafting a clear, concise statement of your leadership purpose. The words in

# Consequences of a Good or Bad Culture

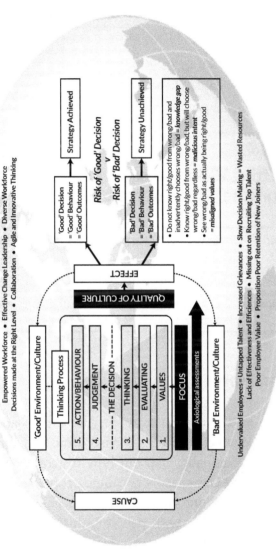

Talent Retention • Broad Mutual Trust • Servant Leadership
Empowered Workforce • Effective Change Leadership • Diverse Workforce
Decisions made at the Right Level • Collaboration • Agile and Innovative Thinking

**'Good' Environment/Culture**

Thinking Process

5. ACTION/BEHAVIOUR
4. JUDGEMENT
- - - - - - THE DECISION - - - - - -
3. THINKING
2. EVALUATING
1. VALUES

FOCUS

Axiological assessments

**'Bad' Environment/Culture**

QUALITY OF CULTURE

EFFECT

CAUSE

'Good' Decision
= 'Good' Behaviour
= 'Good' Outcomes → Strategy Achieved

*Risk of 'Good' Decision
v
Risk of 'Bad' Decision*

'Bad' Decision
= 'Bad' Behaviour
= 'Bad' Outcomes → Strategy Unachieved

- Do not know right/good from wrong/bad and inadvertently chooses wrong/bad = *knowledge gap*
- Know right/good from wrong/bad, but will choose wrong/bad regardless = *malicious intent*
- See wrong/bad as actually being right/good = *misaligned values*

Undervalued Employees = Untapped Talent • Increased Grievances • Slow Decision Making = Wasted Resources
Lack of Effectiveness and Efficiencies • Missing out on Recruiting Top Talent
Poor Employee Value Proposition Poor Retention of New Joiners

your purpose statement must be yours; they must capture your essence and must call you to action. Here are some examples:

My leadership purpose is...:

- Overcoming impossible challenges
- Eliminating chaos
- Creating brilliance

---

## Setting Vision, Mission and Purpose: Three questions

| | |
|---|---|
| *People* | Are you able to keep your work commitments to colleagues? |
| *Task* | Does your team stick by its decisions? |
| *System* | Do your projects have a sense of optimism and a belief that things will work out? |

## Summary

As a leader, you must guide your organisation to create three distinct elements – vison, mission and purpose– and intentionally map out how to work to each of their associated Dimensions of Value: people, task and system. These should inform and support each other, and increase your connection with people by using them to structure your communication. Understand that setting vision, mission and purpose is not an isolated initiative, but will be regarded as such unless you also build the necessary culture to align and support it. Follow the 9 Performance Pathways and then use the Vision Alignment Model to co-ordinate all the moving parts and align the workforce to the vision, mission and purpose.

You have already covered one-third of the steps necessary to build a good culture; there are six more to follow.

| 1. Trust | 2. Team Synergy | 3. Vision, Mission & Purpose |
|---|---|---|
| World Self | World Self | World Self |
| 4. Responsibility & Integrity | 5. Getting Results | 6. Strategies & Discipline |
| World Self | World Self | World Self |
| 7. Innovation & Change | 8. Preparation & Tactics | 9. Consistency & Conformity |
| World Self | World Self | World Self |

# 6

# Pathway 4: Instilling Responsibility And Integrity

## Responsibility and Integrity defined

Leaders must create an environment where everyone feels responsible and accountable for their choices, with a clear understanding of their roles.

## Responsibility

Definition: 'something that it is your job or duty to deal with'; 'to have a duty to work for or help someone who is in a position of authority over you'.[74] For example, Paul has direct responsibility for the induction of the new starters. It is Paul's duty to ensure the new starters receive an appropriate induction; he needs to take ownership of his obligations and he is likely to be held liable for any failures in this area.

## Integrity

Definition: 'someone's high artistic standards or standards of doing their job, and that person's determination not to lower those standards'; 'the quality of being honest and having strong moral principles that you refuse to change'.[75] When somebody has integrity in doing their job, that person displays determination not to lower their high standards, eg 'Lucy was keen to preserve her integrity at work and she refused to take any shortcuts or cut corners.' A more colloquial definition is 'Integrity, the choice between what's convenient and right', as defined by Tony Dungy, the American football coach.[76] That said, this definition does assume that people know what's right in each situation and have the ability to select it within their current environment.

# Why is Responsibility and Integrity the fourth of the nine pathways?

The Responsibility and Integrity Pathway is a combination of the practical day-to-day task elements, such as having clear job descriptions in place, blended with an interpersonal/people dimension value. As explained, there is a mathematical hierarchy in the three value dimensions, from intrinsic down to extrinsic and then systemic. Responsibly and integrity are primarily rooted in extrinsic value, with a secondary element of intrinsic value. They are therefore of slightly lower value than the preceding three steps, which were rooted mainly in intrinsic value.

Hartman discovered that all value has scientific order based on transfinite mathematical sets. In doing so, he identified the principles which order and structure our moral decisions and our value judgements. Hartman's discovery has meant that by using the same value framework to define 'good', we are able to understand how an individual sees and values something through their own valuing lens, which subsequently drives behaviour. The mathematical and logical structure of value concepts is the cornerstone of Axiology.

Hartman devised a way to break down every evaluation we make in to three specific dimensions that could be identified both philosophically and mathematically.

When we think of a loved grandparent – they are unique. How many properties do they have? They have an infinite number of properties. Do they have long hair, brown eyes, wear glasses etc. This means the properties are nondenumerably infinite. They have had children who have had offspring. This is the rule of being a grandparent. This is finite – either someone is a grandparent or they are not.

Both responsibility and integrity rely on the actions and motivations of an individual. To assess these, we need to introduce an expectation. This is 'accountability': 'the fact of being responsible for what you do and able to give a satisfactory reason for it or the degree to which this happens.'[77]

## Why is accountability so important?

Here are three reasons why life as a leader will be easier with more accountability in your team:

1. **Less blame.** Accountable people devote less time and energy to blaming each other. Imagine a day when you don't have to deal with blame stories. Accountability starts with 'What can I do?'

2. **Saves time.** Accountable people own their roles and this fosters a sense of authority and pride. They are then more likely to be proactive, which in turn reduces the need for leaders to motivate, micromanage and intervene to sort out problems and identify what's not working. A team with accountability is more self-sufficient. For the leader, that's less time spent cajoling and coddling. This relies on individual role-awareness, through clearly defined roles and responsibilities.

3. **Less conflict.** When there is no accountability, conflict smoulders in the wings; resentment can last for years as people wait for acknowledgements and apologies that are hard to come by. Accountable people consider how they might have played a role in the issue and are therefore willing to step forward to fix or improve the situation.

Greater accountability isn't just a nice attribute for a team to have; it makes a real difference to organisational results.

Here are three areas that benefit from having higher levels of accountability:

1. **Better customer service.** Think about your worst personal Customer Service experience. Did they listen to you, show concern and ask questions to understand your issue? Or did they blame colleagues or other departments? Did they try to push the blame back on to you for causing the problem? Did you get repeatedly passed from one department to another?

2. **Higher productivity.** The evidence is clear: accountable people get more done. When you raise accountability, you increase productivity.

3. **Higher quality.** Quality improves when people take ownership and are accountable for their work and results. Even the best processes cannot overcome a lack of accountability in an organisation.

The case for accountability is clear, so why is it so thin on the ground? All too often in our consulting work, we hear leaders expressing their frustration at the lack of accountability in their team. We hear the same questions time and again: 'How can I increase accountability in my team?'; 'Why aren't people accountable anymore?'; 'How can I create accountability?'

This third question holds a clue to the apparent scarcity of accountability – it cannot simply be 'created' or 'applied' to an organisation. You can't simply hold a team meeting and announce that 'from Monday, you will all demonstrate greater accountability.' As a leader, you can't simply 'install' accountability in your staff, nor can it be learned by attending a training session or a series of exercises. Accountability is not a behaviour that can be instructed, such as 'smile when you greet a customer', nor is it a set of prescribed responses that can be handed out as a script to call centre staff to follow. Accountability is a state of mind – an attitude – and it requires you to have the right motivation to think responsibly. It is a cognitive process that needs to become an ingrained habit, and that requires a cultural shift. For this move towards greater accountability to take place, the workforce needs to be fully engaged and empowered and have adequate self-esteem and competence to follow through on action. Unfortunately, the pandemic has made this harder: 'Following a steady rise over the last decade, employee engagement decreased globally by two percentage points, from 22% in 2019 to 20% in 2020.'[78] In Western Europe, only 11% of the workforce reported as engaged, but averages don't tell the whole story. The engagement levels in the region ranged from 22% in Iceland to 5% in Italy. The maths is worrying; it means that most employees are not engaged. This fall in engagement explains why accountability has also dropped: you need to have a positive attachment to your work to feel accountable.

Even if you don't feel engaged in your work, personal integrity may remain. It's more of an individual attribute, more intrinsic, which means it just 'is'. Here are three reasons why integrity is important:

1.  Leading with integrity means you listen to your heart, follow your gut instinct and do what you believe to be right. Your actions are transparent as is your motivation – you did what you felt was right.

2.  When you act with integrity, you win other people's trust (especially close colleagues), people feel more comfortable in your presence and you gain influence. This is crucial for leaders who need to demonstrate that they are dependable and accountable for their actions.

3.  Integrity is a hallmark of ethical leadership. Companies, clients, colleagues, stakeholders and communities want leaders that they can trust. When you demonstrate integrity, you show everyone that you can be trusted and respected. You become a role model.

## How to build the Responsibility and Integrity Pathway

As a leader, you first must lay the foundations as set out in the preceding three chapters:

1.  Building Trust and the Common Bond

2.  Building Team Synergy

3.  Setting Vision, Mission and Purpose

If you have not successfully addressed these first three steps, you have not prepared the environment, provided the reasons or crafted the clarity to facilitate overall heartfelt accountability.

## The Responsibility and Integrity Pathway in the three value dimensions

|  | *Strengths* | *Toxicities* |
|---|---|---|
| *People* | Must be capable of independent, autonomous and responsible actions | They would not worry about ownership for their mistakes and inappropriate decisions |
| *Task* | Must pay attention to doing the right thing | They would not be concerned about doing their best |
| *System* | Make certain the consequences of his/her actions reflect standards | They would not worry about the consequences of their actions |

## Create the right environment

You need to create an environment that fosters responsibility and integrity. Ask yourself these key questions:

- Intrinsic value – Do you have a sense of inner responsibility and the ability to clearly identify principles and codes for making ethical, honest decisions?

- Extrinsic value – Do you have the ability to respect and protect company property and does your environment enable you to do so?

- Systemic value – Do you value and respect company rules and regulations allowing consistently honest decisions?

# Who do you need to be to build Responsibility and Integrity?

This is a case of 'Be the change you want to see', a quote thought to derive from a passage by Mahatma Gandhi.[79] This phrase reminds us of our responsibility in bringing about change. Be a role model, lead from the front and 'walk the walk'. This demands certain behaviours.

## Keep your promises

Be careful what you promise. Don't commit to doing things for your team that you can't be confident you can deliver. Speak precisely to avoid 'casual overpromising, unshared truths, vague requests and vague commitments.'[80] If you keep rearranging individual or team meetings, this is an example of failing to keep your promises. When you allow yourself to be distracted or interrupted when talking to a team member, it sends a message that you are not respecting their time and breaks the promise you implicitly made when you agreed to a discussion with that person.

## Demonstrate your accountability

If an issue or problem falls within the accountabilities of your area or your job description, own it. Don't seek to shift responsibility to others, whether within the team or in other departments, and certainly don't lay the blame on the organisation's overall strategy. Acknowledge accountability as you accept praise – where it is due.

## Respect standards and principles

Ensure your projects pay attention to established standards and maintain a high moral framework.

## Be trustworthy

Trust is the first step, as we covered earlier. If you have not managed to build a team culture where there are high levels of mutual trust, you won't be able to make team members feel comfortable and supported in taking responsibility for their mistakes. It is easier for people to acknowledge accountability when they are already aware of the potential results of, or repercussions from, their admissions and they are willing to accept these. Uncertainty breeds anxiety and fear. When people don't feel comfortable and supported, they will hold back on taking the lead in and decision making for fear of negative consequences and ramifications if they were to fail. They become indecisive and cautious, wasting time double-checking and reworking their thought processes. They consult with colleagues, to check their decision and potentially also to share the potential liability, and too often they will still decide to delegate upwards to have the decision signed off, no longer willing to take this responsibility alone.

As a leader, this is a problem. Supporting your employees in making the necessary decisions will often come to dominate your one-to-one interactions with your team members. Your calls and conversations become 'issues based' and hand-holding, and you can end up firefighting when crucial decisions have been skirted around or delegated unnecessarily. You will also become overwhelmed by the volume of emails into which you are copied. The 'cc' function of email is a plague; team members use it in a variety of ways, one of which is to cover their own back. If something goes wrong, they can always fall back on their 'cc' emails to avoid accountability: 'Well you were copied in on the email, and since I didn't receive any feedback, I thought there were no issues so I went ahead.' If this sounds familiar, go back to the chapter on trust and work through the necessary steps to build trust in your team.

## Tools to help you build Responsibility and Integrity

---

### TOOL: THE RACI MATRIX

As a leader, you will often have several different projects running simultaneously. To work efficiently, team members need to know what's expected of them, and there should be total clarity on who is responsible for what.

Richard uses the RACI matrix to identify roles and responsibilities within teams to reduce the risk of confusion during projects.[81] This tool is a responsibility assignment chart first introduced in the 1950s, the name an acronym for the four questions that must be answered about any project:

- **R**esponsible: This considers which person or role is responsible for ensuring the work needed to complete the task is done. Generally, this is one person who has overall responsibility for getting the job done or decisions made, although others may assist or support.

- **A**ccountable: This identifies the person who is accountable for the completion of the task. This is the person who must approve the work and to whom the 'responsible' person is answerable. This is often a senior leader or project sponsor. No task should have more than one accountable person; single-point accountability is the cornerstone of precise project control.

- **C**onsulted: If required, these are the people identified to provide information, knowledge and expertise for the project. Often, these are subject matter experts.

- **I**nformed: If required, these are those who need to be kept informed of project progress. These are the ones affected by the outcome of the tasks or project.

### How to create a RACI matrix

1. List all the tasks needed to deliver the project on the left of the matrix diagram.
2. List the project roles across the top.
3. Complete each cell by writing who is responsible, who is accountable, who will be consulted and who will be informed for each task. Do not leave any blank cells.
4. The finished RACI matrix is an important document to share with all parties involved in the project.

| Project Initiation | Project Executive | Project Manager | Business Analyst | Technical Architect | Application Developers |
|---|---|---|---|---|---|
| Task 1 | C | A/R | C | I | I |
| Task 2 | A | I | R | C | I |
| Task 3 | A | I | R | C | I |
| Task 4 | C | A | I | R | I |

As a leader, you can use the RACI matrix and model to discuss, agree and communicate roles and responsibilities. However, this alone is not enough; it's one thing to clarify a team member's responsibility, but another to ensure that they are truly committed.

---

## TOOL: JOB DESCRIPTION CHECKLIST IN THE THREE DIMENSIONS OF VALUE

Job descriptions tend to have a heavy bias towards accountabilities and practical tasks. They focus on the What. We advocate that you build job descriptions that are underpinned by all three value dimensions, to provide the Who, the What and the Why.

Try to ensure your job descriptions address each of these points:

**People points (intrinsic) – Who**

- What are the cognitive tendencies needed for the role? For example: strong in empathy, integrity, creativity; innovative; proactive thinking; problem-solving skills; expert at planning and organisation; an ability to build positive working relationships; good at delegating and working with others; keen on compliance; able to see the big picture.

- Note, this list is all about thinking skills and not behaviours. People need to think to do their jobs; you can't behave your way to resolve an issue or land an opportunity. This is even more prevalent in a virtual environment where individuals are on their own for long periods of time. This is why all hearts, hands and heads on deck aligned with purpose will keep people thinking and behaving on target.

**Task points (extrinsic) –** *What*

- Job title: Bear in mind that titles mean different things to different people so offer a clear explanation. Include relevant department information and specify who the position reports to.
- Description of duties: Outline specifically what is expected of the person fulfilling the role. Start by identifying the essential activities; list the most important key results and responsibilities. Include outcome measures that indicate how to meet expectations and reach goals. Use key performance indicators to explain how the success of the job will be measured.

**System points (systemic) –** *Why*

- Purpose: Why does this job exist? Make clear the connection of this job to the vision, mission and purpose for the team and organisation.
- System standards: Outline relevant principles, standards, legislation and rules that need to be observed.

---

### TOOL: INTEGRITY BUILDER – LIVING BY YOUR WORD

Never undermine your behavioural integrity by giving the wrong message, even unintentionally. Perhaps you casually offered to 'do lunch' but never got round to it, or you promised support to a new starter who was struggling but then never found the time and quickly forgot. Remember that, as a leader, your words carry weight and employees will remember what they regard as broken promises. Speak precisely to avoid inadvertently making promises or issuing vague commitments. Strategies and techniques to ensure clarity in communication include:

- Clearly state the parameters of your authority.
- Speak the truth no matter how awkward.
- Have commitment conversations: ask for what you want deliberately and with clarity. Make specific commitments in return. 'Honest negotiation'[82] generates more significant levels of trust. Refer back to the commitment conversation framework covered in Pathway 2: Team Synergy.

---

## Responsibility and Integrity: Three questions

| | |
|---|---|
| *People* | Do you feel comfortable and supported by the broader organisation when taking responsibility for your mistakes? |
| *Task* | Do you reinforce others' personal commitment to do what is right? |
| *System* | Do your projects pay attention to established standards? |

## Summary

Responsibility and integrity are not easy qualities to instil in others. An isolated drive and campaign to increase responsibility and integrity within your organisation will not work. The ability to exercise responsibility and integrity every day has to develop from, and be maintained by, the right environment and culture, and once you have it, it is an essential contributor to organisational success. Many organisations have recognised the growing need to be agile and adaptive; however, this can only be achieved with a workforce that knows what to do, wants to do it, always does the right thing, and takes ownership for making it happen.

We have covered four of the nine pathways and can already see how these foundations build a good culture. In the next chapter, we explore the Getting Results Pathway.

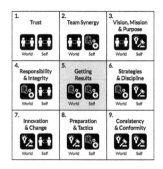

# 7
# Pathway 5: Getting Results

## Getting Results defined

The Getting Results Pathway is all about focusing on the outcomes first, then finding innovative ways to accomplish them. Every organisation has its own definition of success, and this chapter will explore how to create the pathway to great results.

We don't need to spell out why results are essential. A myriad of books tackles the holy grail of 'results delivery' via various tools such as 'balanced scorecards',[83] 'Big Hairy Audacious Goals' (BHAG),[84] key performance indicators and triple bottom lines.[85] Results are defined and delivered at individual, team, departmental and organisational levels. Results can be the tangible or intangible output of an action, each action the results of many decisions. The quality of thinking dictates the quality of the decisions, and determines the actions and therefore the quality of the result. Leaders must create a culture that values, fosters and enables people to produce and share good-quality thinking, guided by a shared vision, mission and purpose.

## Why is Getting Results the fifth of the nine pathways?

We know that there is a mathematical hierarchy in the three value dimensions, intrinsic at the top, extrinsic and systemic value at the bottom. The actual process of getting results is rooted purely in extrinsic value. It's all about the real world, in real time, paying attention to properties, parts, and steps, and measuring, weighing, comparing and processing the environment.

## How to build the Getting Results Pathway

As a leader, you first must lay the foundations via the first four pathways:

1. Building Trust and the Common Bond

2. Building Team Synergy

3. Setting Vision, Mission and Purpose

4. Instilling Responsibility and Integrity

If you have not yet successfully addressed these four steps, you cannot create the environment, provide the reasons, craft the clarity of direction, or develop an expectation of responsibility and integrity, all of which are necessary for getting sustainable results.

Results can only be achieved if the intended outcomes for individuals, teams and organisations are first clarified; these outcomes should be driven by the stated vision, mission and purpose. The last chapter provided a checklist to improve job descriptions in line with the three dimensions of value, and the RACI matrix to clarify accountability across a team. Let's assume that the desired outcome for a team is clear. We now move on to consider implementation and execution. The challenge for the leader is to equip their teams to develop innovative ways to reliably and efficiently achieve the desired results.

## The Getting Results Pathway in the three value dimensions

|  | Strengths | Toxicities |
|---|---|---|
| People | Must be realistic and honest with self about what they can do | Could not be counted upon in both the good times and bad |
| Task | Must be able to get things done | Would tend to have difficulty in actually getting things done |
| System | Must be able to set priorities that will integrate all needs | Would not be willing to do whatever it takes to accomplish their goals |

## People: Getting Results

The boldest goals are both challenging and compelling, often high effort, but promising great rewards. These outlandish ambitions are euphemistically called BHAG, 'stretch goals' or 'moonshot', referencing the Apollo 11 project to put a man on the moon.[86] Richard worked for leaders who delighted in the art of being unreasonable. Their driving philosophy was that if you aim for the moon and miss, you should at least manage to land among the stars. While this may seem an admirable and inspirational concept, motivating people to work towards goals that might seem improbable or even impossible, it also sets them out to fail unless the goals are broken down and guidance is provided on how to achieve them. Goals are generally handed down from the top to the bottom of an organisation, but to be successful, they require teamwork at every level.

As a leader, you need to create a progressive environment that encourages ambition but always remains rooted in realism. When people feel unable to voice their concerns or doubts for fear of negative consequences, the team will encounter problems – and opportunities for constructive input is missed. We've covered the foundations for creating environments free from fear in the previous four chapters. If you are struggling with repeatedly failing to achieve goals that are ambitious but ultimately unrealistic, you need to go back and put in place the foundations necessary for a good culture. Honesty is the best policy. It's the key to becoming an authentic leader who gets results in an achievable and sustainable way.

## Task: Getting results

What do you need to work on? It all boils down to getting things done. As a leader, you need to persistently marshal the energy to consistently attain your goals. This requires more than just a to-do list and a Gantt chart or two.[87] Here are six areas to consider:[88]

1.  **Goal Directedness:** The ability to be excited about and committed to goals, to muster the energy to push towards attainment of goals.

2.  **Results Oriented:** The ability to pay attention to the achievement of results and to decide to what extent attaining results is a major factor pushing one to action.

3.  **Self-Confidence:** The ability to develop and maintain inner strength based on the belief that one will succeed.

4.  **Self-Attitude:** The ability to utilise a positive self-attitude as a motivating source to push oneself to action.

5.  **Persistence:** The ability of an individual to maintain direction despite obstacles and to stay on target regardless of circumstances.

6. **Consistency:** The ability to maintain a sense of constancy and continuity in one's actions, to be reliable in the transfer of thinking to action.

## System: Getting results

The leader must be able to set priorities that will integrate all needs. The classic tool for managing time between competing priorities is the Eisenhower Decision Principle and the resulting matrix.[89]

This principle derives from a 1954 speech delivered to the Second Assembly of the World Council of Churches by US President Eisenhower. Quoting a 'former college president' of the Northwestern University in Evanston, Illinois, where the assembly was taking place, Eisenhower famously remarked, 'I have two kinds of problems, the urgent and the important. The urgent are not important, and the important are never urgent.'[90]

Eisenhower demonstrated how tasks could be categorised and prioritised depending on their relative urgency and importance. He recognised that we must spend our time on important things, not just on the immediately urgent. 'Important activities have an outcome that leads to us achieving our goals, whether these are professional or personal, whereas urgent activities demand immediate attention and are usually associated with achieving someone else's goals.'[91] This means that we often find ourselves turning to urgent activities first, even though they may not be connected to our long-term goals, simply because the negative consequences of not dealing with them are immediate.

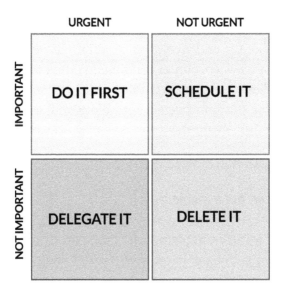

## How to use Eisenhower's Principle to help you manage your time

List the activities and projects that you feel you must do. We recommend categorising them under three headings corresponding to the three dimensions of value: people, task and system. Then use the strategies described below to schedule your activities.

### 1. Urgent and important

Urgent and important activities need to be completed immediately. There are two distinct types of urgent and important activities: those that you've left until the last minute and those that you could not have foreseen.

You can eliminate last-minute activities by planning your time efficiently and avoiding procrastination. However, you will always encounter unforeseen crises or issues that couldn't have been predicted or avoided. The best way to prepare for the unexpected is to block out some time in your schedule every day to handle any unexpected problems as they arise.

## 2. Important but not urgent

These activities complete essential work and help you achieve your personal and professional goals. Make sure that you leave plenty of time to do these things properly and do not leave them to become urgent; remember to allow contingency time to deal with unforeseen problems. This will maximise your chances of staying on track, and help you avoid the added stress of work becoming more urgent than necessary. It is worth scheduling dedicated time for these activities so that they do not slip.

## 3. Not important but urgent

Urgent but not important tasks prevent you from achieving your goals. A common source of such activities is other people; sometimes it's appropriate to politely say 'no' when asked, or encourage them to solve the problem themselves.

These activities can often be rescheduled or delegated. An excellent way to do this is to arrange regular meetings with those who interrupt you often so that you can deal with all their issues at once. Alternatively, try to have dedicated time slots when you are available so that people know when you are available to speak with them. By collating interruptions and delegating where possible, you'll then be able to concentrate on your important activities for longer.

### 4. Not important and not urgent

These activities are just a distraction – avoid them if possible. You can simply ignore or cancel many of them, and others may be OK as long as the time spent on them is carefully managed.

Some may be activities that other people want you to do, even though they don't contribute to your own desired outcomes. Again, say 'no' politely, and explain why you cannot do it. If people see that you are clear about your personal objectives and boundaries, they will often avoid asking you to do 'not important' activities in the future.

## Who do you need to be to build the Getting Results Pathway?

To build the Getting Results Pathway, you will need to develop several key skills as a leader.

## Able to exercise pragmatic judgement

You need to develop clear, pragmatic judgement and be consistent in applying it every day. This means developing the ability to investigate a situation, quickly identify the key details, properties, parts and steps, and then sort out the critical issues. If this incisive approach is not a natural strength for you, find a project manager with a highly pragmatic skill set who can focus on providing you with the right evidence to make informed decisions and so build your pragmatic judgement.

## Able to stay in touch

You must make it your business always to be in touch with what is happening, able to form accurate assessments and act when appropriate. This requires you to be proactive and inquisitive.

Create good habits by using the five reflection questions (outlined in Chapter 5 on Setting Vision, Mission and Purpose) to sum up your and your team's week and plan ahead. By reflecting on the good stuff that you have achieved, you are going to be more confident of tackling the hard challenges in the week ahead. This is even more important in the hybrid world since it will help people draw a line under their working week.

Use the three dimensions of value to structure how you keep in touch.

- **People:** Ask questions and seek feedback on what is going well and what is not. Don't rely on the chain of command for this information; go to the 'shop floor' to find out how they see it on the ground. Talk to your customers and suppliers.

- **Task:** Check projects are on track via tracking metrics and milestones. Put in place regular status reviews.

- **System:** Check for alignment to the strategy, purpose, mission and vision. Are standards and procedures being consistently followed?

## Able to avoid analysis paralysis

Get used to making decisions without spending too long gathering data. Avoid any tendency to hesitate too long before acting. It's about establishing momentum. Ask yourself: When is good enough, good enough?

# Tools to help your Getting Results Pathway

---

### TOOL: CONSIDER WHAT TRULY MOTIVATES YOUR TEAM

When putting in place strategies to motivate your team to deliver results, are you confident that you truly understand how each individual is motivated? Leadership has moved way beyond 'carrot and stick'. Leaders need to integrate the motivational needs of their team members into their plans.

We now understand that motivation is more complicated than historically understood. The assumption used to be that money was the primary source of motivation. Through Axiology, we have now identified six motivation factors, both internal and external. These cover a person's attitude toward service, material possessions, recognition and status, personal development, sense of mission, and sense of belonging.

**The six motivating factors:**[92]

1. **Service:** The importance of seeing, appreciating and meeting the needs and interests of others.
2. **Money and material things:** The degree to which money and material wealth are important to an individual.
3. **Status and social self-recognition:** The importance of receiving recognition and reward via awards, plaques, accolades and other forms of distinction.
4. **Personal development:** The importance of a well-designed plan for one's career development.
5. **Sense of mission:** The degree of commitment to personal ideals, goals and principles.
6. **Sense of belonging:** The importance of being a team member and working in a comfortable place where one is liked, accepted and valued.

---

## TOOL: HOW TO INTEGRATE THE NEEDS OF ALL STAKEHOLDERS

Projects often fail because they have not considered the views of a sufficiently broad range of stakeholders. Taking the time to consult widely is key: although it may feel like progress is slower initially, engaging and canvassing input from more people than might seem necessary facilitates swifter implementation. A project delivered collaboratively encounters less resistance and is more likely to succeed.

How can we understand what consultation is necessary and who should be asked?

1. The first step is to work with your team to create a list of all the people who might need to be involved in approving, supporting or implementing your project or initiative. You'll be surprised, as the list of names is likely to be longer than you think.

2. Now note down what you know about your key stakeholders. You need to know enough to estimate their likely feelings and attitude towards your project. In his book *The 7 Habits of Highly Effective People*, Stephen Covey's 'Habit 5' sets out a powerful communication message that echoes the anonymous 'Prayer of Saint Francis':[93] 'Seek First to Understand, then to be Understood.'[94]

3. To understand your stakeholders, ask yourself the following questions:
   - What interest do they have in the outcome of your work? Is it positive, neutral or negative?
   - What motivates them most of all?
   - What information do they need?
   - How do they want you to communicate?
   - How will you win them around if they are likely to be negative?
   - How will you manage opposition?

4. An excellent way to answer these questions is to ask your stakeholders directly. Asking people's opinions is often the first step in building successful relationships. People are often quite happy to share their views, and asking shows that you value their opinion, whatever that might be.

5. Having received the responses, you should then classify each stakeholder as described in the table below.

| Stakeholder Classification | Description |
| --- | --- |
| Sponsor | Sponsors are individual decision makers who have the authority to legitimise a change effort. Sponsors have a decision-making role for critical change elements. They are typically leaders of highly-impacted stakeholder groups. |
| Advocate (Champion) | Individuals and/or groups who have a vested interest in the success of the change. Advocates are most interested in realising the expected benefits and should be well positioned to leverage their internal influence and relationships for the project's benefit. Advocates often act as 'cascading' sponsors. |
| Change Agent | Represents the highly-impacted areas in the business. They are the people responsible for managing and reinforcing the change. Responsibilities may include shaping solutions; championing and guiding aspects of the project; coaching and preparing sponsors and leaders; helping prepare users and frontline staff for implementation; and managing benefits realisation. |
| Target (End User) | Individuals or groups who are highly impacted by the change are therefore the central focus of the change effort. If uncertain about the role a person has, always treat the person as a potential target until proved otherwise. |

6. Next, consider the stakeholder's commitment level using this framework. It's best to do this formally in MS Excel.

| Stakeholder State | Description |
| --- | --- |
| No Awareness | Does not know that the project is taking place. |
| Awareness | Encounters the project and realises change is imminent. Does not fully understand what the impact will be. |
| Understands | Accepts the nature and intent of change from the project. Knows when the changes will take place and the impact on them. |
| Acceptance | Actively discusses the benefits of the project and demonstrates a willingness to embrace the new ways of working. |
| Commitment | Articulates the changes as new norms and expresses their ownership of the project. Participates in facilitating the project changes. Modifies behaviour or procedures to support process changes post-implementation. |
| Curiosity | Does not yet understand the specifics of the project but is supportive of the impending change. |
| Resistance | Understands the project but does not support it. |

7. Now that you have completed the identification and analysis stages, it is time to develop your stakeholder engagement strategy. Document the results of your analysis in a spreadsheet that lists each stakeholder's category and commitment level.

8. Equipped with this clear analysis of each of your stakeholders, you can now decide how to engage them in your project and how best to communicate with them. You can also identify any specific objectives and input you require from them.

9. Finally, you can decide on your communication plan. How will you engage each person? The diagram below outlines several possible methods, divided into indirect and direct methods of communicating your project.

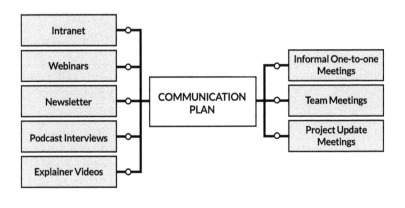

---

## TOOL: PLAN AND PRIORITISE THE DAY IN REVIEW

Planning each day and reviewing your results at the end of it is a critical step in evaluating, setting and adjusting your priorities. Devote time each day, first to plan and then to review your day. The results will be stunning!

Ask yourself the following questions, noting down your answers:

- What were my top three priorities for today and did I achieve them?

- What are my top three priorities to accomplish tomorrow?
- How will your priorities lead to your goals?

---

### TOOL: PERSONAL THINKING VALUES

 If you'd like to purchase access to an online thinking exercise which will only take you fifteen minutes to complete, and give you an accurate report on your personal thinking values, helping you understand your strengths and potential development areas. Scan the QR code or follow this link: *www.catapult-solutions.co.uk/shop*

---

## Getting Results: Three questions

| | |
|---|---|
| *People* | Are you free to be realistic and honest about what you can achieve? |
| *Task* | Does the team take care of the daily detailed work and get things done? |
| *System* | Are the priorities of your projects agreed upon collaboratively? |

## Summary

The right environment and culture are required to support the delivery of results. Going to your team and imposing challenging demands, with the expectation that they will do whatever is required to deliver, will not get sustained results unless you have first created an appropriate environment, as we have outlined. Innovation leadership and innovative problem-solving skills are likely to become more critical than ever in the challenging times ahead. Honesty, ambition tempered by realism and the ability to prioritise and get things done are the cornerstones of a pragmatic leader.

We have covered five of the nine pathways, and we are beyond the foundation stage of building a good culture. In the next step, we explore Pathway 6: Success Strategies and Discipline.

# 8

# Pathway 6: Developing Strategies And Discipline

## Strategies and Discipline defined

The ability to develop successful strategies and strong personal discipline are the key skills required to identify potential obstacles and blocks and develop solutions to overcome them. It is the ability to track and measure the success and failure of decisions.

Every organisation has its own definition of what success means for them. We covered this in Pathway 3: Setting Vision, Mission and Purpose. Pathways 4 and 5 developed the ideas of responsibility, integrity and accountability and also explored ways of getting results. We now move on to consider how to ensure success.

## Why is Success Strategies and Discipline the sixth of the nine pathways?

Strategies and discipline are primarily rooted in extrinsic value with a secondary basis in systemic value. It's therefore a combination of pragmatic judgement, combined with conceptual (systemic) thinking.

In the previous chapter, we covered Getting Results. However, life is not linear: the unexpected lies around the corner and cannot always be foreseen, however carefully we plan the future. To quote Robert Burns' poem 'To a Mouse':[95]

> But Mousie, thou art no thy lane,
>
> In proving *foresight* may be vain:
>
> The best laid schemes o' *Mice* an' *Men*,
>
> Gang aft agley,
>
> An' lea'e us nought but grief an' pain,
>
> For promis'd joy!

Putting it into today's language, Burns tells the mouse that despite the greatest of plans, things will often go off the rails through no fault of your own. This experience is universal, as Burns notes, as foresight and planning will sometimes fail us, whether 'Mice' or 'Men'. Or, from a military perspective: 'No plan survives first contact with the enemy' (in the words of Prussian Field Marshall Helmuth von Moltke the Elder, 1871).[96]

As an aside, the word 'strategy' derives from the Ancient Greek στρατηγός (*stratēgós*), which means 'general, commander of an army'. It is fitting that the role of the general – a leader of plans and adaptations – has morphed into what we call 'strategy' today.

## How to build the Developing Strategies and Discipline Pathway

As a leader, you first must lay the foundations via the preceding five pathways:

1. Building Trust and the Common Bond

2. Building Team Synergy

3. Setting Vision, Mission and Purpose

4. Instilling Responsibility and Integrity

5. Getting Results

We live in a world rife with volatility, uncertainty, complexity and ambiguity. As a leader, you are responsible for many of the decisions that define how your organisation operates. The pandemic, growing environmental concerns and geopolitical developments have all increased the VUCA nature of the rapidly changing world. In response, you must maintain the discipline of continuously scanning the horizon and putting plans in place to deal with the inevitable barriers that will block your path to success, while recognising that foresight is fallible. This means that agile thinking is now more necessary than ever before: 'Best practice was yesterday; best thinking is in demand today and tomorrow.'[97]

## The Success Strategies and Discipline Pathway in the three value dimensions

|  | Strengths | Toxicities |
|---|---|---|
| People | Must seek feedback from others to improve performance | Would not put the interests of the team above their personal priorities |
| Task | Must be able to identify obstacles and find ways to overcome them | Would not think ahead and have a Plan B in case things did not work out |
| System | Must plan for things not working out as expected | Would not consider the consequences of 'shooting from the hip'; would tend to be more reactive than proactive |

## People: How to encourage feedback

Over to Richard:

> During my time at a breakfast cereal company, we introduced the practice of having 'fireside' chats with colleagues. It was straightforward and highly effective. In pairs, we sought feedback from each other using the 'Stop, Start and Continue' structure outlined in Pathway 1:

- What would you like me to *stop* doing?
- What would you like me to *start* doing?
- What would you like me to *continue*?

The only permitted response to the feedback was 'thank you', nothing more; any further discussion could lead to a debate which too often included excuses, explanations and justification from the person receiving the feedback, rather than the simple acknowledgement demanded. The pair then switched roles and asked the same three questions of the other.

It may seem simplistic, but it made a big difference. For example, my boss had a habit of answering the phone every time it rang, even if we were sitting in his office mid-discussion. It was a habit that we had all tolerated, but it meant that what should have been a fifteen-minute discussion between an employee and our boss invariably ended up lasting an hour, as we waited for him to finish his call. When it came to my fireside chat with the boss, I cited this as my wish for his 'stop doing' feedback, and to his credit, he stopped answering the phone during meetings from that point onwards. Initially, he still reached for his phone, but then he would look across and smile. This willingness to act upon feedback strengthened the team's respect for the leader. It also enabled an increase in efficiency that was welcomed by all. It also strengthened my conviction that there is no point in asking for feedback unless you are going to act upon it.

A second example of a good way to seek feedback is via role play. When I was a national sales manager at a breakfast cereal company, we used role play to prepare for negotiations. It proved invaluable since it enabled us to get feedback from others on how we made decisions, acted, responded and behaved and then modified our behaviour accordingly. There is no doubt that this strengthened the negotiation skills of the whole account team and our success in actual negotiations increased. It also enabled richer debrief sessions after customer meetings since we could now compare how the actual negotiation had played out compared to the role play negotiation and identify how we could have improved our performance.

## Task and System: How to build a success strategy using barrier thinking

Most leaders tend to adopt a 'can-do' attitude and their plan is designed to land 'wins'. Sounds reasonable? Sorry, but there's a problem: this conviction means that all too often potential pitfalls are not identified in advance and optimism replaces realism. These leaders don't plan for when things don't work out as expected. How can you avoid this trap? Here's a personal story from Richard.

I was introduced to an incredibly effective alternative way of building a successful strategy. It's called barrier thinking, and it encourages a 'can't do' attitude in place of the blithe certainty that can get leaders into trouble. In short, once the, vision, mission and purpose of the project are set, the next step is to list all the potential barriers that could prevent you from reaching your desired goal.

Barrier thinking is central to the management philosophy of Idris Jala who was a mentor to one of Richard's former bosses at Shell, Asada Harinsuit. After Idris left Shell, he agreed in December 2005 to become CEO of Malaysia Airlines. His mission was to turn the failing airline around, a feat that many considered impossible. The airline was in financial crisis, with only enough cash to last three and a half months. In the first year under Jala's leadership, the company was able to break even, and in the second year, they made record profits. Idris's approach was to bring all the problems to the surface rather than allowing them to fester away beneath the carpet. Shining the light on problems, encouraging people to talk openly about issues and then investigating their root causes increased focus, transparency and accountability. Once the problems were understood, the next task was to build a plan to overcome each barrier. His success strategy was created from a series of initiatives to mitigate each risk in turn to reduce their potential impact. You can see how a plan that is designed in this way is likely to do well.

Barrier thinking is an approach derived from the world of safety and risk management. It works by identifying potential hazards and then putting human or engineering 'barriers' in place to prevent that from happening or to mitigate the consequences. How can you apply Idris's barrier thinking approach in your organisation? Let's consider this using Axiometrics®, specifically the three thinking patterns of people, task and system. When building your success strategy, consider these questions:

| People | Which people could prevent us from achieving success due to a lack of the necessary skills or knowledge, or more worryingly have slipped through the recruitment process and are a poor cultural fit and they are unable to access their talent? Have we not had a colleague who, on paper, looks brilliant, but their attitude sucks which has a negative impact on everybody else? |
|--------|--------|
| Task | What processes or technology within the business will prevent us from achieving success? |
| System | What rules and structures within the business will prevent us from achieving success? |

Ask your team these questions and encourage them to be brutally honest. Unfortunately, most organisations have a strong blame culture, overt or concealed, that prevents the truth from surfacing as it would if they had a foundation of honesty and trust. You can use barrier thinking successfully if you have first developed the necessary team and cultural characteristics outlined in the earlier pathways.

---

### TOOL: THE KPI DISCIPLINE – HOW TO KEEP ON TRACK

Idris has another core discipline called 'anchoring on the chosen KPI'. He believes that it is fundamental that you first identify the correct key performance indicators (KPIs) needed to be able to measure your success. He thinks that people take this crucial step too lightly and often adopt KPIs without fully understanding what constitutes success for their organisation. He advocates boiling things down to a tight core of KPIs. Ask yourself, 'Do you currently have a cottage industry of reporting? Do you face a bewildering bank of KPIs?' If so, you need to take a hard look and identify the cornerstone or driving KPIs that influence the other measurements. Focus your attention just on a short set of these foundational KPIs. It's far more realistic to expect to keep track of a short set of KPIs than to hope to monitor a busy dashboard of metrics.

Within this short set of KPIs, it's essential to identify the leading indicators. Monitoring these leading indicators gives you advanced warning of likely performance. In sales, for example, it's critical to monitor the size of the sales pipeline and understand the conversion rates. If the number of qualified sales prospects falls below normal levels, you can then predict that this will reduce sales in the coming weeks or months. The leader must monitor this KPI to anticipate this problem and take remedial action to head off what's coming around the corner: the leader can ask the team to detect what has caused the drop and work with the team on actions to boost the number of qualified prospects.

---

# Who do you need to be to build the Success Strategies and Discipline Pathway?

## Track and measure your decisions

Many people make decisions and move straight on. This is a mistake. You need to follow and measure the success and failure of your decisions. It's not possible to track all outcomes in your head so you'll need to adapt or create a system to monitor the quality of your decisions.

You can't track every single decision. As noted earlier, we continuously make many small decisions on autopilot thanks to having formed habits; some estimates are that more than 40% of people's actions each day aren't actual decisions but simply habits.[98] For example, you don't consciously decide which gear to select and how to move the gearstick, you just change gear. It therefore only makes sense to track the decisions that lead to measurable outcomes. For example, hiring a new team member, making a purchase or making any business decision contributes to a trackable KPI. It's important to record your decisions and note down the key reasons for making the decision you did, plus any associated assumptions. Write down your points under the three headings of 'people', 'task' and 'system'. You will remember from the five-step decision-making process introduced in Pathway 2: Team Synergy that the second step, 'Evaluating', involves considering a decision against the value dimensions. By tracking the factors contributing to your decisions under these three headings, you will gain an understanding of any potential bias by seeing how evenly the points are distributed across the three value dimensions. This will help you understand the preferences or biases at play in your decision-making process, in addition to tracking the success or failure of the decision that resulted.

## Commit to undertaking post-implementation reviews

In projects which require many decisions, it is instructive to hold a post-implementation review (PIR). The purpose of this is to evaluate whether you met the project objectives, determine how effectively the project was run and assess the quality of decision making. In addition, the aim is to learn lessons for the future and ensure that the organisation gets the most maximum benefit from the project. We cover this in more detail in Pathway 9: Consistency and Conformity.

## Who not to be: three things to avoid

Taking the spirit of barrier thinking and applying it to consider who you need to be, here are three tendencies to avoid which could self-sabotage your success as a leader. Bear these tendencies in mind at all times and actively take steps to avoid:

- Not always being open to admitting mistakes; be willing to accept when you are wrong and change directions if required

- Making commitments that are unrealistic and impossible to achieve

- Being unwilling to take risks when required, for what you believe is right

# Tools to help you build Success Strategies and Discipline

Over to Richard:

At Shell, we had a rigid discipline and process to manage risk which we reviewed quarterly in our leadership team. As I discovered, the sources of potential risk are far more numerous than you might think. We took a whole management approach to assessing and quantifying risk.

The discipline of plotting each risk involved the whole management team. Each risk was assigned a single owner at the leadership team or board level, and they would report on the risk status and provide updates on their respective mitigation plan. A second board member would then challenge their assessment to test if the risk description was robust. This process brought a cross-discipline approach and pooled the collective knowledge, often generating a clearer understanding of each risk from the discussion. Ongoing peer assessment of risk also helped each leader to gain a sense of scale about the relative danger of each risk. It allowed each person to become far more confident and quicker at distinguishing between crisis issues and minor problems. Over time, the ongoing risks became better managed; new risks that inevitably appeared were assessed by the same process.

We used a risk matrix for plotting our risks, with the two axes defined as 'impact' and 'probablity', on a scale from low to high.

# Five Step Decision Making Process

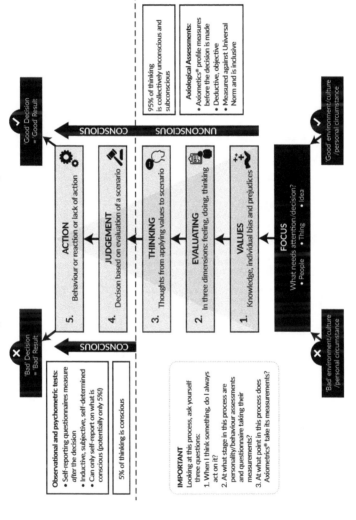

'Good Decision = 'Good Result'

'Bad' Decision = 'Bad' Result

**CONSCIOUS** (right arrow)

**UNCONSCIOUS** (left arrow)

**CONSCIOUS** (left arrow)

95% of thinking is collectively unconscious and subconscious

**Axiological Assessments:**
- Axiometrics® profile measures before the decision is made
- Deductive, objective
- Measured against Universal Norm and is inclusive

'Good' environment/culture /personal circumstance

'Bad' environment/culture /personal circumstance

**5. ACTION**
Behaviour or reaction or lack of action

**4. JUDGEMENT**
Decision based on evaluation of a scenario

**3. THINKING**
Thoughts from applying values to scenario

**2. EVALUATING**
In three dimensions: feeling, doing, thinking

**1. VALUES**
Knowledge, individual bias and prejudices

**FOCUS**
What needs attention/decision?
- People
- Thing
- Idea

**Observational and psychometric tests:**
- Self-reporting questionnaires measure *after* the decision
- Inductive, subjective, self-determined
- Can only self-report on what is conscious (potentially only 5%)

5% of thinking is conscious

**IMPORTANT**
Looking at this process, ask yourself three questions:
1. When I think something, do I always act on it?
2. At what stage in this process are personality/behaviour assessments and questionnaire taking their measurements?
3. At what point in this process does Axiometrics® take its measurements?

## TOOL: THE RISK MATRIX

Write down your organisation's risks under the following categories:

*Financial risks*

- Capital market risk
- Credit risk
- Market risk (competitor, substitution, customer)
- Interest rate risk
- Foreign exchange risk
- Price risk
- Liquidity risk

*Other risks*

- Country risk
- Health, safety, security, and environmental risk
- Political risk
- Property and liability risk
- Technology risk (eg cyber security)
- Intellectual property risk

When considering risk, there are two main aspects to review:

1. What is the chance of the risk occurring?
2. What would be the impact of the risk, should it occur?

On the **'impact'** scale, the typical classifications used are, from low to high:

- *Trivial*: Risks that bring no negative consequences or pose no significant threat
- *Minor*: Risks with little potential for adverse consequences; unlikely to jeopardise success
- *Moderate*: Risks with negative consequences that pose a moderate threat to success
- *Major*: Risks with negative effects that will impact the success
- *Extreme*: Risks with extreme consequences that could cause failure

On the '**probability**' scale, risks are assessed as:

- *Rare*: Infrequent risks, with virtually zero chance of happening
- *Unlikley*: Risks that are uncommon and have a tiny chance of happening
- *Moderate*: Risks with a 50/50 chance of occurring
- *Likely*: Risks that are very likely to occur
- *Very likely*: Risks that are virtually certain to occur

When plotting each risk on the matrix, an arrow indicates if the risk has changed since the last risk review meeting.

### Classifying and prioritising risk

After plotting each risk in the matrix, you allocate each one an overall ranking. Rankings combine the impact and probability to help determine which risks pose the most significant threats and are therefore the top priority to address. High probability risks with severe negative consequences will receive the highest rank; low impact risks with low probability rank the lowest.

Rankings generally fall under a few broad categories, which are often colour-coded:

- *Low* (yellow/light grey in diagram): The consequences of the risk are minor and unlikely to happen. These risks are generally ignored.

- *Medium* (amber/medium grey in diagram): Somewhat likely to occur, these risks carry some more concerning consequences. Take mitigating steps to prevent medium risks from happening but remember that they are not high-priority and should not significantly affect success.

- *High* (red/dark grey in diagram): These are serious risks that carry significant consequences and are likely to occur. Prioritise and respond to these risks in the near term.

Once you've ranked your risks, you can then create a risk response plan to prevent or mitigate those that are 'high' or 'extreme'. Each risk is then represented by a coloured dot indicating their status:

- Red: no mitigation in place

- Amber: mitigation not yet completed

- Green: robust mitigation plan in place

|  | | IMPACT | | | |
|---|---|---|---|---|---|
|  | Trivial | Minor | Moderate | Major | Extreme |
| Rare | Low | Low | Low | Medium | Medium |
| Unlikely | Low | Low | Medium | Medium | Medium |
| Moderate | Low | Medium | Medium | Medium | High |
| Likely | Medium | Medium | Medium | High | High |
| Very Likely | Medium | Medium | High | High | High |

PROBABILITY

## TOOL: HOW TO CREATE EFFECTIVE FEEDBACK IN ANNUAL APPRAISALS

Annual appraisals are traditionally the occasion when leaders focus on providing feedback to their employees; unfortunately, this is often also the only time that some leaders offer feedback. We'll deal with that issue shortly, but before that, we want to share the most effective set of five questions that we've encountered when conducting annual appraisals:

When you look back at this year, consider how you would answer these five questions:

1. What have you achieved this year?
2. What went well?
3. What did not go so well?
4. What did you learn?
5. What's going to be your focus for next year?

Richard explains:

I used to send these questions out to the team member in advance; this prompted people to dedicate some quality time to reflect on the past year. This five-question structure always prompted a high-quality discussion and allowed me to provide feedback as their team leader. This also set the stage for the coming year: I had a licence to provide immediate feedback if I saw somebody doing something that they had decided in the annual reflection to do differently.

I went through the same reflection format with my boss and the effect of using this annual reflection routine across the entire organisation helped to foster a culture of feedback.

## Success Strategies and Discipline Pathway: Three questions

| People | Do you consistently seek feedback from others to improve performance? |
|--------|----------------------------------------------------------------------|
| Task | Does the team track the outcome of decisions, both successes and failures? |
| System | Do your projects develop strategies for crisis intervention? |

## Summary

Aim for a clear mission and adopt a healthy 'can't do' attitude. Use barrier thinking to help you anticipate what can go wrong and establish plans to deal with the potential issues. The discipline of the risk matrix is an excellent method of applying the barrier mindset. Monitor cornerstone KPIs. Seek feedback from colleagues, both informally and formally, but also commit to act on the feedback. Tracking the success and failure of your decisions will help you learn and improve your success rate. *Best thinking* is what you need for the future.[99]

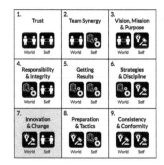

| 1. Trust | 2. Team Synergy | 3. Vision, Mission & Purpose |
|---|---|---|
| World  Self | World  Self | World  Self |
| 4. Responsibility & Integrity | 5. Getting Results | 6. Strategies & Discipline |
| World  Self | World  Self | World  Self |
| 7. Innovation & Change | 8. Preparation & Tactics | 9. Consistency & Conformity |
| World  Self | World  Self | World  Self |

# 9
# Pathway 7: Fostering Innovation And Change

## Innovation and Change defined

The Innovation and Change Pathway is all about creating a culture that encourages, supports and rewards innovation and evolution. It requires an adaptive growth model that encourages trial, error and learning.

## Innovation

The word 'innovation' comes from the Latin verb *innovare*, which means 'to change, to renew'.[100] Today, innovation still retains these meanings, but it is generally accepted that the change will be an improvement on, or a positive replacement of, what has gone before. Innovation is not confined to significant game-changing inventions or revolutionary new products; it occurs at many levels. It can be a new process, a novel way of marketing, or an everyday improvement to make things simpler, more affordable or more efficient. Innovation, in many situations adds more value. In the public sector, innovation can mean new ways of managing organisations (eg via public–private partnerships or initiatives), new ways of rewarding people or new ways of communicating, such as via WhatsApp or other social media platforms.

Some innovations are so fundamental that they become systemic. For example, the creation of the NHS or the move to a low carbon economy. Innovation often begins with a prompt or trigger that makes shift possible or demands change. Sometimes innovation is forced – by a crisis, cost pressures or political demands, and sometimes it is catalysed by new technology. The pandemic has given most organisations no option but to innovate and adapt to survive.

## Change

Change is a constant in our VUCA world. The word 'change' is derived from the Old French (c. 1200) *changier* ('to alter; exchange; to switch').[101] Today, it is defined as 'to exchange one thing for another thing',[102] and in business, this is generally understood as a process in which a company or organisation varies its working methods or aims in response to new situations and to develop.

# Why is Innovation and Change the seventh of the nine pathways?

Innovation and change are primarily rooted in systemic value, with a secondary intrinsic value basis. It's, therefore, a combination of conceptual (systemic) thinking and intuitive (intrinsic) thinking.

## Why is innovation important?

To increase their competitiveness, companies can do one of two things: they can strive for price leadership, or they can develop a differentiation strategy. In both cases, innovation is essential. Companies that choose price leadership must secure their long-term competitiveness by introducing changes that increase efficiency and economy, to cut costs and improve the quality-of-service delivery and therefore increase the profits. To do this, product and process optimisation and continuous improvement in terms of costs are essential. Companies that strive for a differentiation strategy need innovation to develop unique distinguishing features to mark them out from their competitors and meet the rising expectations of their consumers. Consumers are becoming more powerful and increasingly expect a seamless bespoke experience, personalised to meet their specific needs and with evidence of innovation.

Innovation is not just important within business and commerce. Governments and public service organisations and under increasing pressure from social, geopolitical, economic, environmental, legal and technological factors which mean that evolution is the only way to survive and remain current in the VUCA world. Governmental bodies are also facing rising expectations, as private citizens increasingly expect their public services to offer answers to their concerns, demonstrate accountability and raise the quality of their output to meet the consumers' record-high expectations. Ongoing growth and development are necessary just to keep pace, as existing methods and solutions will not meet the new challenges and increased demands.

## How to build the Innovation and Change Pathway

As a leader, you must lay the foundations to build a good culture by following the preceding six pathways:

1. Building Trust and the Common Bond

2. Building Team Synergy

3. Setting Vision, Mission and Purpose

4. Instilling Responsibility and Integrity

5. Getting Results

6. Developing Strategies and Discipline

Richard worked for twenty-five years in global corporations, including a seven-year stint in Research and Development (R&D); over that time, his view of innovation has broadened. He doesn't see it restricted to significant, game-changing inventions or new products.

Innovation occurs at many levels. It can be a new process, a novel marketing method or an everyday improvement to make things simpler or more affordable. Innovation brings so many benefits. Yet, businesses are still not getting the impact they want, with studies showing that '94% of executives are dissatisfied with their firms' innovation performance,'[103] despite investing heavily in innovation incubators, accelerators and initiatives. Why is this the case? The answer is simple: they have not first created the right culture. Without building the necessary foundations, innovation will fail. It is not a 'behaviour' that can be taught, but a cognitive capability that can only be nurtured within an appropriately supportive environment.

We know from our work on the value dimensions that culture is key to innovation, and this is confirmed by research: the 2011 annual global study by Booz & Company showed that 'companies with both highly aligned cultures and highly aligned innovation strategies have 30 percent higher enterprise value growth and 17 percent higher profit growth than companies with low degrees of alignment.'[104] It is clear that those companies that have established a good culture that aligns with the strategic goals and supports innovation are at a significant advantage compared to their competitors.

An innovative culture values and enables thinking diversity; environment shapes performance. Richard has worked in an organisation that perpetuated a 'good news culture', where delivering bad news was discouraged. While this could seem like an optimistic and supportive strategy initially, ultimately it led to an environment that stifled innovation. By not allowing employees to share their failures as well as their successes, people did not want to put their heads above the parapet and became reluctant to take risks and explore new ideas and innovation. An evidence-based culture that only attaches value to ideas from those with an established and solid track record of success does not encourage invention more widely.

If new and creative ideas are regarded with suspicion if not supported by a comprehensive business case, and there is a tendency to regard their inventors as pipe-dreamers, this is not a culture that encourages the risk taking required for innovation. When your blue-sky ideas are repeatedly shot down, this damages self-esteem, as Richard can testify. Once your self-esteem becomes fragile, you can't be your best, and your ability to innovate and create is restricted. Too often innovative ideas never take off simply because their creators work within an environment that has not given them the confidence needed to share their ideas, or assured them of their worth and the value of their contributions. Sometimes even psychometric assessments and reports can damage this confidence: if they are given a label that is not associated with innovation or creativity, they can form a self-limiting belief that they are not good at innovation. For example, in DISC, if you are labelled as D (dominant) you are told that one of your perceived weaknesses is that you are uncreative. If you have been given D as your badge are other people likely not to include you as part of a problem-solving team? And yet, innovation is a cognitive thinking capability and not a behaviour, as DISC and other psychometrics report to measure.

Innovation comes from empowered people working in teams that have high mutual trust. You can't force innovation to happen in one-off meetings or use a template to create an invention. It needs to be tended and nurtured in a trusting environment that fosters thought diversity and all the characteristics covered in the previous pathways.

## The Innovation and Change Pathway in the three value dimensions

|  | Strengths | Toxicities |
| --- | --- | --- |
| People | Must promote confidence in others to take risks | Would not have an interest or inclination toward ideas and strategies for improving themselves |
| Task | Must be open to ideas for solving problems | Would not be able to keep perspective or become too focused on seeking new or inventive solutions |
| System | Must know when to take risks and make changes | Would not be open to inventive thinking and would tend toward being closed-minded |

## People: How to promote confidence in others

What type of innovation happens when R&D scientists don't have to worry about building a business case and are instead trusted and given the freedom to spend time discussing new ideas and given access to resources to support their experimentation? 3M is an example of a company where this has been done successfully and which has consequently developed a strong culture of creativity, interdependence and collaboration.

In 1948, 3M launched a scheme that gave their scientists the freedom to spend 15% of their paid time pursuing pet projects, using company resources.[105] One of the scientists involved in a company project to produce a strong glue sang in a local choir. He found it frustrating when the pieces of paper he inserted to mark the songs in thick hymnbooks kept falling out and fluttering to the floor. His mind raced back to the glue project and he had an idea: the project had failed to deliver the powerful glue that they had been looking for, but it had created a light adhesive that would be sticky enough to keep the bookmarks in place but without damaging the books' pages; so the Post-it Note was born, and the rest is history.

If leaders have worked through the previous six pathways in turn, they can now, with credibility, loudly encourage their people to 'fail-fast' and demand to see 'the size of your scrap heap'.[106] In other words, rather than proceed cautiously and slowly, they can encourage their people to undertake bold experiments that quickly prove their viability and then ask to see evidence of the failures: if you have not failed enough, you have not been pushing the boundaries hard enough. While this carefree approach to risk taking can be liberating, we have also seen leaders use this rhetoric without success; this is usually because trust has not been in place first, and innovation has not been fully integrated into the vision, mission and purpose. If failing fast, learning from experience, and feeling confident and free enough to express yourself without fear of being judged are part of culture throughout your organisation, you have developed an environment and good culture that supports innovation.

Let us consider a case study from Richard.

In the early 2000s, I was responsible for managing the multimillion-dollar R&D programmes for several downstream product businesses. In an attempt to increase productivity, the leaders of the sponsoring businesses put in place stringent business case requirements. To obtain funding for an R&D project, we had to develop commercial viability, backed up with projected increases in sales, market penetration and cost savings, and projected returns on the budget investment.

You can imagine what happened next. The scientists with the most unconventional and creative ideas could not provide the necessary input or data to help me build a business case that would stand up to scrutiny. The more innovative and potentially exciting the idea, the harder it was to provide accurate milestones and timelines for programme delivery; we were simply dealing with too many unknown factors. I remember my frustration when imploring my technical colleagues to give me the details I needed to build a business case to support their proposals; the most common answer to this was an evasive 'it depends' – it became a mantra.

Across the R&D site, there was a tense atmosphere. The businesses had been cutting funding year on year. At that time, innovation was not part of their purpose, mission and vision and there was an obvious lack of strategic alignment. Their focus was on cost reduction so there were regular rounds of redundancies, team synergy went out of the window, and people understandably wanted to secure their own positions so trust fell. A step designed to boost productivity in R&D had created an environment that inhibited innovation.

## Task: How to be open to ideas

Fight the urge to react negatively, dismissively or even angrily when you hear differing opinions. Instead, take a moment to yourself. Remember, we all think in different ways, and it is our thinking that drives our decisions and actions. Adopt a position of genuine curiosity and ask open and inviting questions such as 'Why do you think that?', to probe their thinking further.

Don't be afraid to ask a lot of questions. First, explain to your colleague why you are asking so many questions and explain that it is to gain a better understanding. If you don't explain your motivation, they may feel that you are interrogating them as part of a judicial process and their willingness to open up and share will decrease. Be willing and eager to listen and practise active listening: focus on the person speaking, and resist the urge to interrupt. Remember to consider your own bias when noting your response as you listen. What is driving your thoughts? Consider your thinking process before landing on your position and avoid speculation or jumping to conclusions.

## System: Know when to take risks and make changes

In the context of organisations, risk means that an organisation's plans may not pan out as intended or may not meet its target or achieve its goals. Be honest about what could go wrong. Use barrier thinking to actively plan how to mitigate risks rather than being tempted to ignore them. Consider potential bad outcomes, determine their likelihood and decide what you would do next. Don't ignore hazards or possible problems but instead think about how you would handle them and plan appropriately.

It is worth noting how you feel about each risk; your anxiety level usually has nothing to do with the actual level of risk you face but simply how you perceive it. Take glossophobia, for example, the fear of public speaking; it's believed to affect up to 75% of the population to some degree, and is the top fear for many,[107] but let us for a moment rationally consider the actual risk that this poses. While there may be elements of a public performance like this that cause you anxieties and therefore feel unpleasant, the chance that you will be in mortal danger is near zero. Acknowledge your emotional response but balance it with a logical examination of the facts to assess the actual level of overall risk posed by public speaking. Consider the risk matrix tool introduced earlier: while the chance of an 'acceptable' risk such as you experiencing nerves is 'possible', the chance of a 'catastrophic' outcome such as death from stage fright is vanishingly unlikely. List the pros and cons of each possible decision and the potential risks versus benefits. Writing down the points and viewing the risks will help you achieve balance.

When you're excited about an opportunity and worry that you're likely to overlook or underplay the risks, ask a mentor, friend or colleague to help you think through the potential downsides. Talking through the potential drawbacks and unwanted ramifications can help you become more rational and ensure decisions are made by the head and heart, not just heart alone.

# Who do you have to be to build Innovation and Change?

There are two sides to the people conundrum of creating an innovative culture. First, as a leader you need to be able to lead innovation. Second, you individually and collectively need the thinking talents to solve problems.

## An innovation leader

Innovation leadership is the capacity to inspire and influence others, to enlist their co-operation and resources to achieve a goal. It requires three areas of focus: creativity is necessary to ensure that the product or service is extraordinary or new; leadership supports the talents of, and guides, the people who make things happen; strategy provides direction to the people and process.

- **Creativity** is the ability to be open to new options and ideas and apply inventive optimism to problems and challenges that move a group forward.

- **Leadership** is the ability to make decisions while promoting the freedom of others, motivating them to take risks and be accountable for achieving the shared mission.

- **Strategy** is the ability to think into the future and decide proactively, setting challenging goals infused with a strong sense of purpose and priorities.

---

### TOOL: INNOVATION LEADERSHIP CHECKLIST

 We have developed a series of thirty questions, under the headings of the three pillars of Innovation leadership: creativity, leadership and strategy. To access it, scan the QR code or follow this link: *https://www.catapult-solutions.co.uk/wp-content/uploads/2020/03/20200309-Innovation-Leadership-Skills-Individual.pdf*. You will find a series of checklists that invite you to score yourself from 'excellent' to 'poor' across several leadership characteristics, and then poses some additional questions for you to think about further. Scoring yourself is of course subjective and inevitably impacted by your bias, but it is still useful to become aware of and reflect on the necessary characteristics and skills and will provide some indications as to who you are as an innovation leader.

---

## Supportive of innovative problem solving

Every time we close the gap between where we are and where we want to be, we engage in problem solving of some sort. Sometimes the solution is obvious, eg to turn the light on, we flip the switch; sometimes it is not so obvious, and the lamp fails to work. Our VUCA world has seen many changes which means that familiar things and processes that we used to rely upon no longer work in the same way.

There are four steps critical to innovative problem solving:

1. **Problem definition:** Identifying the problem to work on; establish key facts and collating information; generating related problem statements; collecting the best problem statement to meet the goals

2. **Solution finding:** Looking at the problem from different points of view; generating a wide range of possible solutions; selecting solutions based on specific criteria

3. **Implementation:** Translating solutions into actionable steps, which include selling and getting approvals for solutions, testing, measuring and fully implementing the solutions, making adaptations when required

4. **Teamwork:** Using and contributing diverse perspectives; assisting one another to be more effective problem solvers; building individual and team strength while recognising and affirming both contribution and success

You will often find that you achieve the best results when there is effective teamwork. Many different perspectives yield a more precise definition of the problem, a richer field of possible solutions, and insight into the best ways to implement them.

## TOOL: INNOVATIVE PROBLEM-SOLVING CHECKLISTS

See the following links and QR codes for a series of checklists that invite you to score yourself and your team from one to ten on the necessary skills for the four phases of innovative problem solving.

 Innovative problems solving tool for the individual: *www.catapult-solutions.co.uk/wp-content/uploads/2020/01/20200109-Innovative-Problem-Solving-Individual.pdf*

 Innovative problems solving tool for teams: *https://www.catapult-solutions.co.uk/wp-content/uploads/2020/01/2020-Innovative-Problem-Solving%E2%80%94Team-Tracker.pdf*

# Tools to help you build Innovation and Change

## TOOL: THE CHANGE EQUATION

Change can be especially problematic. We can want change but still fear change; change creates stress; and whether imposed on us or self-imposed, change always shakes up the present and brings forth the unknown future. There have been several attempts to formulate change,[108] first in David Gleicher's 'Formula for Change' (often erroneously ascribed to Beckhard and Harris)[109] and then refined and simplified by Kathleen Miller into the 'Change Equation' we know today:[110]

$$C = D \times V \times F > R$$

Where:

- $C$ = **Change**
- $D$ = **Dissatisfaction** with how things are now and desire for a new future: If the path forward seems too hard, there will be no compelling need for change.

  In many circumstances, real commitment and excitement are necessary to cause change. They are an initial source of energy and therefore the power to drive change.

- $V$ = A clear **vision** for the new future: Even though you may feel uncomfortable in your current transition situation, you will find yourself stuck if you don't have a roadmap.

  Individual visions are not enough, they must be shared and seen to be legitimate and desirable.

- $F$ = **First** steps towards that vision: Do you know where to start?

  A sense of where you want to get to is not enough if you can't think of the practical steps necessary to move forward.

- $R$ = **Resistance**: What are your potential issues and concerns at the moment?

  How do you anticipate these blockages and minimise their effects?

  What might be the demotivating factors for your team?

This means that change will only occur when the product of D, V and F multiplied is greater than R, the resistance to change. It is worth remembering that anything multiplied by zero is zero, so if any of these factors is absent, it will not be possible to overcome resistance and the change will not occur. Mathematically, this could be described as

$$C = (D \times V \times F) - R,$$

so change will only be positive when

$$D \times V \times F > R.$$

We can illustrate this with an example. To be successful, the vision for every change needs to be in alignment with the organisation's overall vision. Richard recalls that Shell used to call this change vision 'the case for change'. Shell was primarily a company with a strong combination of an evidence-based pragmatic approach, and rules-based systemic values. Employees were reluctant to change unless the practicalities and strategy had first been laid out; this was an understandable consequence of having so many engineers in the business. Over time, there was a growing recognition that the 'people' story was also needed, to provide intrinsic and emotional value to support the fact-based, rule-based case for change. This addressed the D element of the change equation, the necessary desire to change, which previously had no value. As we know, any value multiplied by zero will always result in zero, so without D, R could not be overcome – the absence of the intrinsic people dimension prevented successful change. The D value increases when the vision, V, is clear and compelling. A strong vision will also increase the value of F, as a clear destination makes it easier to identify the steps necessary to get there.

---

## TOOL: WIIFM, OR 'WHAT'S IN IT FOR ME?'

When planning change, it is important to consider every stakeholder and identify for each the impact, benefits and potential downsides of the plans. Recognise that the stakeholders likely to be affected by your plans will ask WIIFM, so it is important to communicate using all three dimensions of value, ie language which reflects emotional, practical and conceptual needs. As outlined earlier, the discipline of stakeholder management ensures all concerns are understood and addressed.

---

## TOOL: MARKETING DIRECTION – THE THREE KEY QUESTIONS

A well-known marketing question framework plots a course between the current state (Point A) and the desired future state (Point B). To identify the journey, it asks three simple questions:

1. Where are we now?
2. Where do we want to get to?
3. How can we ensure we get there?

---

## TOOL: THE FOUR STAGES OF CHANGE

Throughout our lives, we will all undergo numerous experiences of change and transformation. Accepting and undergoing change can be difficult, even if the change is for the better. Just like individuals, organisations will also undergo numerous changes, both big and small. As a leader, you have a responsibility to manage these changes in a way which motivates your people, and also to understand where people are on the change journey so that they can offer appropriate support to help them through the process.

The Four Stages of Change is a simple model designed to illustrate the four-stage emotional journey that we undertake as we experience change.

Here's an illustration of what people think, say and do at each stage of the change journey:

| | Stage 1 | Stage 2 | Stage 3 | Stage 4 |
|---|---|---|---|---|
| | Status Quo | Resistance | Exploration | Rebuilding |
| *What people think:* | Denial: They deny that change is coming or is necessary. | Anger/fear: They know that they do not want to accept the coming change. | Appreciation: They start to engage with the new situation. | Integration: They integrate the change. |
| *What people say:* | 'It'll never happen'; 'It won't affect me'; 'We've heard it all before'; 'Yes, but...'. | 'I haven't got time for that'; 'It's all their fault'; 'If only they'd...'; 'I can't do that until...'; 'When...'. | 'If we could...'; 'What would happen if we...'; 'If we tried that, it might work?'; 'If I knew how to.....' | 'We can do it'; 'It's easy'; 'We've got the best way of doing it.' |
| *What people do:* | Fail to participate or engage in change discussions; take steps or actions to block or sabotage change; seek evidence to justify their position. | Undermine and complain; gossip and lots of talking by the coffee machine; criticism, accusations and blame; minimal compliance and obvious dissatisfaction; employees become sick or fail to attend. | Explore options; ask questions; become curious; discuss alternatives; try things out. | Embrace the change; take responsibility and participate; suggest and implement; build on experience; make things happen; strive to make the change a success that brings about improvement. |

## Innovation and Change: Three questions

| | |
|---|---|
| *People* | Can you keep an open mind and listen to other people's ideas for solving problems? |
| *Task* | Is your team consistently innovating to improve outcomes? |
| *System* | Do your projects keep perspective and take into account critical issues when innovating? |

## Summary

Spending more and more money on R&D to drive innovation is pointless unless the right culture is already in place. Genuinely innovative organisations have a culture that supports innovation, and this culture can be created by working through all the previous pathways in turn.

As an individual, it is possible to develop your innovative leadership; use the self-help checklist provided in this chapter to help. You can also build the skill level of your teams in a similar manner, to improve their innovative problem-solving ability; again, use the list in this chapter. We live in a VUCA world, and the need to innovate and change has never been more vital. Change is joined at the hip with innovation, and this chapter has provided several tools to help you lead and manage change.

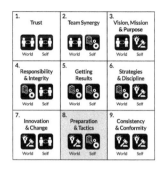

# 10
# Pathway 8: Preparation And Tactics

## Preparation and Tactics defined

This chapter is about personal competence and confidence in making decisions. It has to do with the ability of the individual or organisation to solve problems efficiently and effectively, and the steps needed to make success more likely.

## Preparation

'Preparation' derives from the verb 'to prepare' – 'to make or get something or someone ready for something that will happen in the future',[111] derived from the Latin verb *praeparare* ('to make ready beforehand'), which in turn is composed of two Latin root words, *prae* ('before') and *parare* ('make ready').[112]

## Tactics

The word 'tactics' is derived from Modern Latin *tactic*, from the Ancient Greek τακτικός (*taktitos*). It meant 'of or pertaining to arrangement', especially in the context of war.[113] The modern meaning of the singular noun is 'a planned way of doing something', and in the plural, 'the organisation and use of soldiers and equipment in war'.[114]

Preparation and tactics is about thinking ahead, planning, anticipating outcomes and considering potential problems and the necessary steps to overcome them. The more prepared you are, the more composed you will be in the face of challenges, and as a result, you can make confident decisions and tackle problems calmly and appropriately. Preparation equips you with tactics for firefighting if the potential challenges that you identified in the planning stage come to fruition.

As we head towards the final pathway, we will focus on some essential leadership skills and traits: the art of 'keeping cool' in stressful situations, problem solving in advance and personal competence in planning.

## Why is Preparation and Tactics the eighth of the nine pathways?

Preparation and Tactics are primarily rooted in systemic value with a secondary basis in extrinsic value. It's therefore a combination of conceptual (systemic) thinking, and pragmatic thinking (extrinsic).

## Why are Preparation and Tactics important?

Preparation is the process of planning, and it increases awareness and readiness, but tactics are the action steps required. When you feel prepared and ready, you are confident in your plan and your stress levels are lower as you know that all potential problems have already been considered and addressed. Although we earlier recognised that 'no plan survives first contact with the enemy',[115] now we modify this slightly, to acknowledge that a thoroughly prepared plan can survive, as all potential outcomes should have been already anticipated. Adjusting the course within a plan is far easier than having to begin again from the start when under pressure.

Preparation saves time. It reduces errors, prevents reworking and avoids the elongated thinking time required to work out solutions in the heat of the moment, as opposed to doing this in advance when things may be clearer and stress levels will be lower. A frank way of expressing this is the British Army adage, the 7 Ps: 'Proper Planning and Preparation Prevents Piss Poor Performance'.[116]

Enough said.

# How to build the Preparation and Tactics Pathway

Too often, organisations fail to prepare adequately; perhaps the most significant example of this is in their failure to create the right culture. Most organisations have not worked through the necessary sequence of steps to build their culture; they hope to achieve consistently successful delivery (the final pathway) without first laying down the necessary foundations via the previous seven pathways:

1. Building Trust and the Common Bond

2. Building Team Synergy

3. Setting Vision, Mission and Purpose

4. Instilling Responsibility and Integrity

5. Getting Results

6. Developing Strategies and Discipline

7. Fostering Innovation and Change

As a leader, it will fall to you to ensure the necessary work for each of these pathways takes place. This means that for each member within your team, you must work on addressing their competence and confidence (intrinsic); their ability to build action plans, schedules and timelines (extrinsic); and their skill in knowing what is needed to get the job done (systemic). To understand how best to address this with your people, consider their thinking patterns. Become more objective by standing back from a situation and working out how people are thinking. This will offer a truly profound way of appreciating what is driving a situation and how it might play out, by understanding the cognitive processes at play and how they differ.

## The Preparation and Tactics Pathway in the three value dimensions

|  | *Strengths* | *Toxicities* |
|---|---|---|
| *People* | Must keep composure in stressful situations | Would not be realistic in evaluating their abilities; tend to over/underestimate their abilities to get things done |
| *Task* | Must have good problem-solving ability | Would not be inclined to deliver projects and commitments on time; not inclined to get things done on schedule |
| *System* | Must focus on planning, focusing and priorities | Would not be inclined to take the time to think ahead |

To identify how people are thinking, consider each of the three dimensions of value. Let's look at some examples. These offer an oversimplification but it is nevertheless instructive.

### People-driven thinker

Somebody with a particular clarity for, and a heightened focus on, other people's thinking is frequently likely to rely upon and be driven by their keenly perceptive empathy. An individual who thinks in this way would naturally tend to be concerned about the implications of their decisions on others. For example, when a people-driven manager introduces a round of voluntary redundancies, they would go to great lengths to deal with this as sensitively as possible to help each individual. They have an unconditional acceptance of people's uniqueness without evaluating, judging or critiquing. They believe in people and try to help them achieve their best, often going beyond what other people may think is necessary or appropriate.

## Task-driven thinker

Somebody with a clear and heightened focus on task thinking is frequently likely to rely upon and be driven by their highly practical pragmatism. For example, when a task-driven manager introduces a round of voluntary redundancies, they would ensure that a meticulous and detailed plan is in place to ensure that the necessary reduction of staff numbers is achieved on budget and on time. An individual who thinks in this way would naturally be concerned about the efficiency of sequencing steps and hitting milestones.

## Systems-driven thinker

Somebody with a clear and heightened focus on systems thinking is likely to be thinking further ahead and be driven by concepts and how things fit in a system. An individual who thinks in this way would naturally be concerned about the new structure of the organisation post the round of redundancies and how the business will operate in the future.

# Who do you need to be to build the Preparation and Tactics Pathway?

## A cognitively-aware leader

Understanding thinking patterns is a game-changer for leaders since it enables them to see beneath the obvious surface-level 'personality' differences. By understanding the thinking landscape, you can tune in, understand and appreciate why people act or make decisions in different ways. Rather than focus on behaviours, this approach can help demystify the thinking that is driving the decisions and actions of the person. Once everybody in the team understands the three value dimensions that underpin our thinking, they can recognise their preferences and biases and appreciate their differences from others.

Remember that we do not think in just one dimension, but in all three, with varying degrees of clarity and focus from person to person and from one moment to another. The environment in which we find ourselves has a profound impact on how we think at that moment. As the team leader, you can develop creative environments that foster an understanding of thinking diversity, and encourage an appreciation of the great value that harnessing cognitive diversity can offer to your organisation.

## Embrace cognitive diversity

In general, we give scant consideration to the diversity of thinking patterns across team members, despite the value that we know this approach can provide. The reason is simple: it has not been easy, quick or affordable to recognise cognitive traits accurately. However, understanding how people think is a way to predict how they will perform.

When a team is composed of members with a tendency to think in the same way, the team becomes vulnerable to 'blind spots'. Without the challenges from people who think and see things differently, these will often go unnoticed and as a result, the quality of decision making suffers. This leads to poor performance which inevitably eventually hits the bottom line, and this causes hugely stressful situations. Using conventional personality and behavioural psychometrics will give you no understanding of someone's thinking diversity, only that their self-perception (which may not be accurate) differs from colleagues. On the other hand, when people within a team think differently, to avoid misunderstanding and missed opportunities differences need to be understood and appreciated. A deeper awareness enables people to see beyond superficial behaviours or communication styles and explains why people may draw different conclusions to the same scenario. The thinking diversity of an organisation is perhaps its most powerful asset, and your task as a leader is to make sure this is fully realised.

Lisa Liswood quoted in Deloitte sums up the benefits to be gained from diversity in thinking styles:

'What is needed is an objective approach that allows selection of thinking diversity, irrespective of the body it comes in. As Deloitte's "Only skin deep?" 2011 report says, "it is not enough to create a corporate version of Noah's Ark bringing in 'two of each kind'". What incredible benefits diversity of thought can offer! It is far too valuable for your workers, your organisation, your customers and your consumers not to be embraced, and it is already inherent within your organisation if only you can create the culture that allows it to thrive.'[117]

## Learn to maintain your composure in stressful situations

A significant source of stress in virtual teams comes from interpersonal differences. The breakdown of working relationships can erode engagement levels, slash productivity and affect mental health; it can result in people leaving organisations or culminate in an unfair dismissal or the more oblique constructive dismissal.

How do personal differences come about in the first place? Often, they arise from a poor understanding of the differences in thinking styles. In response to the same situation, two different people have drawn entirely different conclusions about the best course of action, and they both think that they have the correct answer. Both may be intelligent, educated, experienced and logical people, yet they form different conclusions about the right response. Why is this? The answer is that we are each unique. Ironically, our greatest asset – our diversity of thought – also introduces a vulnerability that causes clashes, stress and emotional outbursts.

A leader must remain calm in stressful situations – not easy! If they let their emotions run away, team members take time off due to stress. The manager must create an environment that is good for well-being and mental health. Unchecked emotional outbursts can not only damage individual team members but can be career damaging for the virtual manager. This is particularly tricky for managers operating virtually who have to pick up on the much more subtle social cues visible on screen, and deal with the breakdown of working relationships and personality clashes in their remote teams that might not have occurred had they worked together on site, and would certainly have been easier to address earlier.

The fact is, we all think differently from each other and this should be recognised and celebrated. We need diversity of thinking, and as a leader, it is your task to harness this cognitive wealth. Building your resilience in stressful situations, and ensuring that you always track behaviour back to the thinking pattern from which it emerges, will help you to remain a constant source of strength for your people as the necessary structure grows around you. People's thinking capacities and performance capability will change or be impacted by personal circumstance and environment, and as a leader you need to be cognisant of this and flex your leadership style accordingly.

# Tools to help you build the Preparation and Tactics Pathway

---

### TOOL: THE SEVEN-STEP PROBLEM-SOLVING TOOL

When things go wrong, it is tempting to leap immediately into 'crisis' mode in a frenzy to fix the issue. You might even find yourself 'solutioneering', a buzzword for pitching solutions before first defining the problem they are designed to solve. A better approach is to see the problem as a learning opportunity and adopt a curious mindset. Think like a detective or doctor; the leader must ask a lot of questions to diagnose the problem before they can begin to treat it. There is good news: problem solving and solution finding are skills that can be developed and we will provide the tools.

In Pathway 7: Innovation and Change, we outlined a four-stage problem-solving checklist to help you assess your skills at problem definition, solution finding, implementation and teamwork. This chapter builds upon this by introducing a seven-step problem-solving process. These additional steps will help you look at a problem from different points of view, generate a wide range of possible solutions and finally, select appropriate solutions based on specific criteria.

### Step 1: Define the problem clearly

What exactly is the problem? Define the problem under the three value dimensions. What is the impact of the situation on people, task and system? Ensure that you are truly diving down to ascertain the reality of the situation rather than being satisfied with what may be mistaken first impressions. Ask yourself if you are making any assumptions. If you have asked colleagues for information, don't unquestioningly accept the first answer; follow it up by asking, 'what else?'

Ask this question more than once; it's amazing how many important issues emerge from just beneath the surface when you ask repeatedly. There is no doubt that so much time is wasted when problems are not adequately understood.

### Step 2: What are all the possible causes of this problem?

Remember to look at this through the three lenses: people, task and system, Who can you find who has relevant experience to explain the cause of the problem? Has this happened before? If so, what was the cause? Has this happened in this industry? How and why did it happen? Ask these questions and answer as fully as you can: the better the quality of your answers, the better the odds that you come up with a satisfactory solution.

There is a simple way to improve the quality of your answers, and that is to keep asking 'why?' until you get to the heart of the matter. This idea was formalised into 'The 5 Whys Technique', a root cause analysis method developed by Sakichi Toyoda, a Japanese inventor within the Toyota Motor Corporation, and first published in 1978 in a book by Taiichi Ohno, then Toyota's executive vice president.[118] The idea is that 'by repeating why five times, the nature of the problem, as well as its solution, becomes clear.'[119] It will help you choose between options that should generate many potential solutions, which you should group under the usual headings of 'people', 'task' and 'system'.

### Step 3: Define the criteria you will use to identify a successful solution

How will you measure success? The absence of a clear set of success criteria will prevent you from identifying a truly successful solution. Group each of your criteria under the same three headings:

| | |
|---|---|
| *People:* | What are the implications for, and impact on, all stakeholders – staff, customers, suppliers, general community, shareholders? Ethics? Diversity? |
| *Task:* | What are the metrics and KPIs to be used? Quality targets? Commercial objectives for profit, revenue etc? Customer satisfaction scores? Timeline and deadlines? |
| *System:* | What are the system requirements? What health and safety legislation must you meet? Budget? Alignment to strategy? Compliance with internal policies such as diversity, corporate responsibility, sustainability? Are there requirements for information security and compliance with data privacy? Use of approved suppliers and technology? |

**Step 4: It is now time to generate some potential ideas**

What are all the possible solutions? If you have done a good job following the first three steps, solutions should now begin to emerge. The more possible solutions you can come up with, the more likely it is that you will come up with an ideal solution. Start by asking three screening questions of each solution in turn, based on the three dimensions of value:

| | |
|---|---|
| *People:* | Is it ethical? |
| *Task:* | Will it solve the problem? |
| *System:* | Does it follow the existing rules and make good business sense? |

If a potential solution passes these three tests, then move on to evaluate the solution against the success criteria that you defined in Step 3. You might find that the process of evaluating all the solutions will help you refine the criteria you previously identified for success.

### Step 5: Make a decision

You have just assessed each potential solution against your criteria defined in Step 3. To complete the next step, you need to record your answers for each possible solution. This could be completed in a simple spreadsheet, either using a 'yes/no' scoring, or by using a numerical Likert scale from low to high to score how well each option stacks up against your success criteria.[120] This stage comes with a health warning: you will be answering your own questionnaire, and while this might feel like a scientific decision-making process, it is still a subjective (and therefore biased) evaluation – but at least it is broken down into small steps that you can approach logically and in turn. Doing this will enable you to build a bottom-up view of the problem and avoid high-level sweeping judgements.

### Step 6: Assign responsibility for carrying out the decision

Who is going to do what, when and to what standard? While these questions may seem simple, this step is so important. Successful implementation only occurs when people fully understand what is asked of them, accept that they are accountable and have a well-defined role in implementing the solution on the ground.

### Step 7: Establish a deadline

Set a timetable for reporting deadlines and establish a standard by which to measure whether or not the decision has been successful. A solution without a standard or deadline is merely a discussion or aspiration.

## TOOL: HOW TO IMPROVE YOUR PRIORITISATION AND PLANNING

There is a whole industry developing systems and apps to help you set priorities. There is also a huge swathe of books, coaching workshops, training processes and methods all designed to teach planning. This is because neither prioritisation nor planning are easy and yet both are critical to achieving success.

Here we present a simple approach derived from the world of coaching. The aim is to help you coach yourself into defining and implementing your priorities in both life and work. Life and work are a balance, and it's not as binary as some work–life balance proponents advocate. The two are connected, and your answers to one are always affected by consideration of the other. Begin by asking yourself the following questions (the answers can refer to today, tomorrow, this week or the month):

1.  What are your top three personal priorities? Why?
2.  What are your top three priorities for your business or career, and why?
3.  Who needs to know about and agree with your personal priorities?
4.  Who needs to know about and agree with your business priorities?
5.  How do your priorities line up with your personal values?
6.  What are your long-term life goals?
7.  How will your priorities lead to your goals?
8.  How are you going to make sure that you keep your priorities straight?

### Action items

- Write your priorities in your planner. The point of these questions is to help you learn to focus on what you believe is essential for you to accomplish.
- Check each day to see if you accomplished them. As you refine this practice, you should get to the stage where you are achieving your agreed priorities every day.
- Get in the habit of adjusting your daily priorities to match the most critical issues for you to deal with that day.
- Remember, do the most challenging things first.
- Schedule regular reviews of your answers to ensure they remain valid and relevant. Your priorities in both your personal life and your work may well change, and one will often be affected by changes in the other.

## Preparation and Tactics: Three questions

| | |
|---|---|
| *People* | Are you able to keep your head and composure in stressful situations? |
| *Task* | Is the team able to discover what is causing problems and delegate accordingly positively? |
| *System* | Are appropriate responses identified to deal with crisis issues and minor problems in your projects? |

## Summary

You can learn to become calmer in stressful situations by becoming a cognitively-aware leader. This book will guide you; we have provided tools to help you improve your problem-solving ability as well as your ability to prioritise and plan successfully. If you have worked through the pathways in turn, you will now have completed all the steps required to create a good culture, but how will it last? Good culture needs to be nurtured and protected if it is to survive, so the final pathway is all about achieving the consistency and conformity required to maintain the hard work undertaken so far.

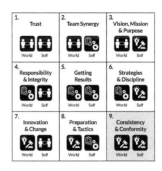

| 1. Trust | 2. Team Synergy | 3. Vision, Mission & Purpose |
|---|---|---|
| World   Self | World   Self | World   Self |
| 4. Responsibility & Integrity | 5. Getting Results | 6. Strategies & Discipline |
| World   Self | World   Self | World   Self |
| 7. Innovation & Change | 8. Preparation & Tactics | 9. Consistency & Conformity |
| World   Self | World   Self | World   Self |

# 11
# Pathway 9: Maintaining Consistency And Conformity

## Consistency and Conformity defined

Consistency and conformity are about respect for authority, rules, codes and property and about establishing goals that are challenging in both the short and long term. Both include an emphasis on the importance of meeting established standards combined with an inherent willingness to do so.

## Consistency

The word consistency is derived from the Latin *consistere*, 'to stand firm'. The meaning 'steady adherence to principles, patterns of action' was recorded in 1716. In modern dictionaries, it is defined as 'the quality of staying the same; loyalty'.[121] For these purposes, we shall understand it as a steady adherence to principles.

## Conformity

'Conformity' derives from the Latin *conformare*, 'to fashion, form, shape; educate; modify'.[122] Over time, this meaning shifted to include an expectation, and today's definition has hardly changed in 500 years: a 'behaviour that follows the usual standards that are expected by a group or society'.[123]

# Why is Consistency and Conformity the last of the nine pathways?

Consistency and conformity are purely rooted in systemic value, the lowest of the three values within the hierarchy. This pathway is therefore all about conceptual thinking, the thinking we use when focusing on rules and working within established principles and standards. Without first working through the previous eight pathways, this conceptual thinking will inevitably fail.

## Why are Consistency and Conformity important?

Leaders who have successfully built a good culture will not want their excellent work to unravel or break down because of a lack of consistency or conformity. A good culture is not a destination, it's a state of being, and there needs to be consistency and conformity within an organisation if it is to build and maintain a good culture and generate the associated high performance and positive results. People need to do the right things in the right way every day, meeting expected standards and respecting the rules if this culture is not to be put at risk.

Consider what would happen if a team member were to make a decision that broke the law; the consequences and ongoing ramifications could be highly damaging to the company as well as the individual. This risk, and others like it, can be mitigated through mandatory training and a register to prove attendance, to ensure that your workers are well acquainted with the necessary systems, processes and regulations within which they must operate, and also understand the potential outcome of their actions. Later in this chapter, we provide a list of crucial regulations and regulatory bodies.

## How to build the Consistency and Conformity Pathway

By this stage, you should already have completed the hard task of building a good culture by following through each of the previous eight pathways:

1. Building Trust and the Common Bond

2. Building Team Synergy

3. Setting Vision, Mission and Purpose

4. Instilling Responsibility and Integrity

5. Getting Results

6. Developing Strategies and Discipline

7. Fostering Innovation and Change

8. Preparation and Tactics

This final pathway is all about learning to maintain the good results achieved so far and keeping the people and culture on track. Systemic thinking underpins this pathway, which is why the emphasis is on rules, standards and goals.

In our discussion of the Innovation and Change Pathway, we discussed the importance of ensuring alignment within a company. Despite this long-standing recognition, too often this is not the case: '36 percent of the respondents to our survey admitted that their innovation strategy is not well aligned to their company's overall strategy, and 47 percent said their company's culture does not support their innovation strategy.'[124] We know that aligned and consistent goals throughout an organisation increase productivity and improve the environment for those within the company, promoting innovation and growth. The goals need to be in line with others within the same project, across all levels, but also consistent with the company's vision, mission and purpose. Systematic goal cascading is a fundamental approach to aligning overall organisational goals to the individual level. To address this, this chapter includes a useful methodology tool.

## The Consistency and Conformity Pathway in the three value dimensions

|  | *Strengths* | *Toxicities* |
|---|---|---|
| *People* | Must be attentive to consequences of solutions | Would not avoid a negative attitude; susceptible to having a 'chip on the shoulder' |
| *Task* | Must maintain a commitment to plans and programmes | Would not be able to avoid making inconsistent decisions |
| *System* | Must respect principles, rules and property | Would not be concerned about making sure that things were done right; quality control would be a low priority |

# Who do you need to be to build the Consistency and Conformity Pathway?

## A consequential leader

Good leaders generate good consequences. They do this through effective planning, thinking ahead and playing out the potential implications of various scenarios and associated decisions to prepare and identify tactics that might be needed. It's akin to considering possible moves, and then various countermoves, in a chess game. It's about having enough certainty in your ability to predict correctly the outcomes of possible actions, but also about having enough power that your instructions carry weight: 'If we do this, then we will achieve a good outcome.' This phrase uses the conditional 'if-then' structure to imply that one thing is dependent on the other;[125] in this case, a good result will be achieved by sticking to the plan. While this may seem straightforward enough, there are two additional elements to consider.

The first is the nature of the relationship between the speaker and the listener. If these words are to have an impact, the relationship between the two must be trusting, confident and mutually supportive. Although there is inevitably a personal element to all human relationships, these individuals are also the product of their environment. Consequential leadership can only succeed in a good culture, where employees are already strongly motivated and inspired, and where co-operation, collaboration and innovation are already well established. It is ideally suited to a culture where:

> 'Everyone meets commitments and holds each
> other accountable, where trust and respect reigns
> and where influence is the only mechanism
> necessary to stimulate safety compliance,
> innovation and business growth.'[126]

In this supportive environment of shared responsibility, leaders can help their colleagues learn to project ahead to consider the potential impact of their actions and identify the barriers that might prevent them from reaching their goals. A firm plan can then be drawn up, with contingencies and barrier planning put in place where needed, a predictive 'if-then' scenario: 'If you follow this agreed path, then it will succeed.' However, inherent within this promise of a reward for compliance is also an implied threat: '*If* you deviate from the path, *then* there will be consequences.'

Leaders must address these implications, these unspoken warnings inherent within the conditional structure. We earlier discussed how fear can stifle innovation, so leaders must ensure that colleagues know and understand the boundaries but without generating a culture of fear or damaging the trust. This means first ensuring that there is absolute certainty and agreement about the intended path, to avoid unintentional departures or divergence. Employees also need to have a genuine understanding of the potential consequences and repercussions of not sticking to the intended path. Where there are potentially severe penalties, leaders must make sure that this is widely understood, to prevent both inadvertent or intentional deviations.

This is the second factor under consideration: the nature of the individuals themselves. We know that it is not possible to know other people completely, but through an enhanced understanding of their thinking, we can come to better predict their potential behaviour. We can also guide them through our 9 Pathways, instilling the values of trust, respect, accountability, responsibility, integrity, empathy and so on. From a practical perspective, the key to keeping your people on track is to ensure absolute alignment to, agreement of and adherence to clear expectations, policies, frameworks and standards. This way, any slight deviations can be detected and addressed at an early stage, before the plan has been affected and before any potentially negative outcomes or repercussions have occurred.

Traditionally, risk management is a key board-level activity. Leaders use risk mitigation to minimise the likelihood of the risk happening and reduce the impact when it happens. Some simple risk management tools should be used to ensure risks are regularly and consistently scrutinised and then addressed. Please see the Success Strategies Pathway for more in-depth coverage of risk management.

## Knowledgeable about current legislation

While an individual will always be held accountable for their actions, as a leader you bear additional responsibilities that extend beyond yourself, to your employees, your organisation and all who contribute at every stage in the delivery chain. You will be frighteningly aware of the enormous fines that can be imposed if your organisation or one of its members breaks a regulatory code, let alone the law. Companies can be fined, businesses ruined, individuals can face financial and personal ruin or even go to jail. To protect you all, you must be totally familiar with current legislation, guidelines and 'best practice', regularly reviewing and revising to ensure your knowledge remains up to date. It is also worth paying attention to current discussions, consultations and concerns, both within your industry and more broadly. This will help you sense any potential shifts that might result in procedural or legislative change in the future or impact your customers' and clients' expectations of where your organisation should be going.

Understanding the scope and breadth of these obligations can be quite overwhelming, but a value dimensions approach will help clarify them, as outlined at the start of this chapter.

Significant legislation that needs to be understood and observed relates to the following areas:

- Promoting fair competition (European competition law, Competitions and Market Authority regulated acts)

- Promoting trustworthy business practices (Data Protection Act (DPA) 2018 and UK General

- Data Protection Regulation (GDPR), Bribery Act 2010)

- Promoting equality of opportunities and diversity (Equality Act 2010, Public Sector Equality Duty 2011)

These acts and regulations are briefly outlined below. Please note: this is a general list of legislation that applies to those operating within the UK; if you are not based in the UK, you will need to check if these apply in your country and also if there are additional considerations. Please also check to see if there have been recent updates or changes.

**European competition law:** 'The competition law in use within the European Union. It promotes the maintenance of competition within the European Single Market by regulating anti-competitive conduct by companies to ensure that they do not create cartels and monopolies that would damage the interests of society.'[127]

There are four main areas of policy:

1. Cartels

2. Market dominance

3. Mergers or takeovers

4. State aid

Since Brexit, the UK has not been subject to the European competition laws.

**Penalty:** The European Commission can impose fines for competition infringement. It considers these fines to be 'both punitive and preventative'. It does not have any powers to impose criminal sanctions: 'While fines are imposed on individual companies, they are calculated at the level of the economic entity, or undertaking, to which the company which has committed the infringement belongs. The legal maximum is 10% of the total turnover of the undertaking as a whole.'[128]

Repeat offenders will be subject to higher fines.

Several of the highest fines issued so far have been to Google, which has been subject to three antitrust penalties: in 2017, a fine of €2.42 billion (the largest fine ever issued at the time), for giving its comparison shopping site an illegal advantage;[129] this was followed in 2018 by the highest fine issued so far, €4.34 billion for illegal practices concerning their search engine;[130] Google was also fined €1.49 billion in 2019.[131]

The highest cartel fine imposed in a single case was related to a fourteen-year collaboration between five truck manufacturers, together representing 90% of medium and heavy trucks produced in Europe. In 2016, Volvo/Renault, Daimler, Iveco and DAF were fined approximately €2.93 billion; the fifth company, MAN, was not fined as it had received full immunity for exposing the cartel.[132]

**Competitions and Market Authority regulated acts:**

- UK Competition Act 1998

- Enterprise Act 2002

- Enterprise and Regulatory Reform Act 2013

Since Brexit, EU competition law is no longer enforced in the UK, and courts are not required to follow EU case law. However, the UK Competition Act 1998 is heavily modelled on European competition law, and previously there was a regulatory duty in place to minimise inconsistencies between the two. So our legal obligations currently remain essentially unchanged, although that is likely to become less true as time goes on.

'Over time, it is expected that more divergence between the two may appear as the UK evolves a competition regime in response to the challenges of the rapidly changing global economy, recovery from COVID-19 and the resulting post-pandemic world.'[133]

**Penalty:** 'We expect the CMA to be very active in antitrust enforcement following the UK's break from the EU. While in the past the CMA (like all national EU antitrust agencies) had to take the back seat where the Commission took up an investigation, it is now able to run an investigation under UK competition law in parallel with an investigation by the Commission and to focus on the UK market specifically.'[134]

Companies can be subject to investigation under both EU and UK competition law, with the potential for fines and penalties to be imposed by both.

**Data Protection Act (DPA) 2018 and UK General Data Protection Regulation (GDPR):** The GDPR 2016/679 is an important regulation outlining privacy and human rights law for citizens of EU member states. It determines the control and rights that an EU citizen has over their own data, both within and outside the EU area. This is the EU GDPR.[135]

In 2018, the EU GDPR was enacted into UK law as the Data Protection Act 2018. Post-Brexit, additional regulations 'amended the DPA 2018 and merged it with the requirements of the EU GDPR to form a new, UK-specific data protection regime that works in a UK context after Brexit as part of the DPA 2018.'[136] This is known as the UK GDPR.

**Penalty:** DPA 2018 and UK GDPR: 'All organisations in the UK that process personal data must comply with these two data privacy laws or risk fines of up to £17.5 million or 4% of annual global turnover – whichever is greater.'[137]

EU GDPR allows fines of up to €10 million or up to 2% of the global turnover of the preceding fiscal year, whichever is the higher; more severe infringements could result in fines of up to double this.[138]

**Bribery Act 2010:** 'It is illegal to offer, promise, give, request, agree, receive or accept bribes.'[139]

The UK Bribery Act prohibits bribery of public officials and business-to-business bribery. Companies are liable in the UK for acts of corruption committed by employees, agents or subsidiaries anywhere in the world.

**Penalty:** 'Any offence under the Act committed by an individual… is punishable either by a fine or imprisonment for up to 10 years… or both.'[140] The sentence is dependent on the severity of the breach.

'A recent judgment in the Crown Court, against a company that had bribed foreign public officials, stated that fines for corruption should be in the tens of millions of pounds or more (R v Innospec [2010]: as per Lord Justice Thomas).'[141]

In 2016, Glasgow-based logistics company Braid Group agreed to pay a £2.2 million fine for breaching the UK Bribery Act 2010.[142]

**Equality Act 2010:** 'The Equality Act 2010 legally protects people from discrimination in the workplace and wider society.'[143]

This law protects individuals against discrimination against nine protected characteristics.

**Penalty:** Cases are brought by individuals who believe they have been subject to discrimination.

'The main remedies available are damages (including compensation for injuries to feelings), an injunction and a declaration.'[144]

**Public Sector Equality Duty 2011:** This is in addition to the obligation not to discriminate already outlined within the Equality Act 2010. It also carries a duty to promote diversity and equality of opportunities and eliminate discrimination.

'Public bodies have to consider all individuals when carrying out their day-to-day work – in shaping pol-icy, in delivering services and in relation to their own employees.'[145]

**Penalty:** 'We work to promote compliance as the preferred option and we usually only take formal enforcement action where efforts to encourage compliance have failed…. If a public authority doesn't comply with the general equal-ity duty, its actions or failure to act can also be challenged through an application to the High Court for judicial review.'[146]

Possible steps include undertaking equality assessments, entering into formal agreements with organisations to increase compliance and intervening in court proceedings where necessary.

## Tools to build the Consistency and Conformity Pathway

---

### TOOL: HOW TO RUN TEAM MEETINGS

Commit to holding regular team meetings. Set them as recurring appointments in everybody's schedule. Put 'people recognition' as a standing agenda item at the start of each meeting; this sets a positive tone for the whole session by recognising the highest of the values, the intrinsic (people) value.

---

Richard became aware of the practice of thanking and recognising colleagues and team members for any particularly noteworthy contributions since the previous meeting and then decided to introduce it into the meetings of the global leadership teams that he led (Marketing, and Learning & Development). For these monthly meetings, they used to rotate the ownership each time. The owner would be responsible for asking their colleagues for agenda topics, building the schedule, issuing any pre-reading, chairing the meeting, running the 'any other business' (AOB) and issuing the action points. Each action would have a single owner and a deadline agreed upon during the meeting. With all leaders given equal opportunities for public praise and appreciation, matched by a responsibility to host the meeting in their turn, all members felt valued and of significance. Allowing the team members to take ownership of the meetings enabled them to feel they had contributed and collaborated in the results and outcomes that appeared. By appealing to the intrinsic value, the team members were able to give their best, and constancy and conformity were more likely as all members were in alignment.

---

### TOOL: HOW TO SET UP A PROJECT

To set up a project successfully, you will have to first agree the Terms of Reference (TOR). The TOR are 'the areas, subjects, etc that an organization or inquiry has been ordered to deal with'.[147] They are crucial for project proposals and need to address four questions: what needs to be achieved, by whom, how and by when. A TOR document needs to contain:

- Information setting out the background for the project, outlining the context within which it is to take place.
- The *what* is addressed by clearly setting out the 'vision, objectives, scope and deliverables'.[148] This section should also present the scope of the work, and what will or will not be included. It considers the outcome intended by the work and the impact this should achieve, and also the overall sustainability of the project going forward. The impact on stakeholders must also be discussed, and any potential resistance or objections that they are likely to

raise identified and addressed. Particularly importantly, it must outline all potential issues, risks and constraints around which the project will be working and suggest possible 'barriers' where they might be needed. Not identifying and addressing potential issues at this stage (the $R$ of the change equation) can lead ultimately to the project failing.

- *Who* needs to be involved and/or consulted about this project? This includes considering what skills, knowledge and expertise are necessary to assist the project, both during its development and implementation, and where within your team these can be found; it might be necessary to consider additional training or external consultation where the skills are not already extant within your team. Decide who will take part in the project, and outline clearly their roles and responsibilities: uncertainty over individual job descriptions is a huge risk within a project, as we discussed in Pathway 4, and makes accountability impossible.

- To address *how* the project will be achieved, we need to consider the methodology required to carry out the plan. It provides 'a set of broad principles and rules from which specific procedures will be derived to define how to carry out the project in a cost-effective way.'[149] It needs to outline the planned process of implementing the plan, broken into specific phases to be worked through in order. From this, various plans can be drawn up to address specific areas within the implementation. These include plans for the various component requirements: resource plans to outline what assets are required at every stage (people, structural, technical, equipment and so on); financial plans to outline the funds required (the budget) and to ensure that they are available at the point where they are needed; and also quality plans to outline how things will be monitored to ensure goals are met at every stage.

- To answer *when* a project will be delivered, we need a firm and defined schedule and a timeline; a work-breakdown structure may be useful,[150] or the timeboxing technique.[151] There needs to be a set completion date, but also several project milestones along the way. It may also be helpful to put in additional smaller milestones, perhaps even for every task or every component, to ensure all involved are given a firm schedule to work under.

- It is also essential to define the governance for the project.

---

Richard notes:

At Shell, these steering groups are called the Decision Review Boards (DRB). The project leader's job is to invite senior leaders from the various areas of a business that will be involved or affected by the projects to join the DRB. The role of this senior group was to make or approve the big decisions. These could involve the commitment of resources or the removal of organisational barriers that might hinder the progress of the project. It might sound bureaucratic, but it is pragmatic. Include a schedule for the DRB meetings in the TOR; it's efficient to have a structure in place to monitor progress and to deal with the unexpected issues that inevitably pop up.

## TOOL: HOW TO REVIEW PROJECTS AND EXTRACT THE LEARNINGS

Conduct a PIR after completing a project, to evaluate whether it met its objectives. If the objectives were met, determine how effectively the project was run, identify things to replicate in future, and consider how to ensure that the project now offers the greatest possible value and remains sustainable and efficient. If the objectives were not met, a PIR enables you to consider why not, and indeed to explore whether the project might be salvageable with changes, or whether it is now redundant.

When you conduct a thorough and timely PIR, you'll identify key lessons learned that you can apply to the planning and management of future projects; this is just as much the case with an unsuccessful project as one where all the objectives have been achieved. Here's a checklist for the questions to ask in a PIR.

### Determine whether the project goals were achieved

- Is everything working as expected?
- Are error rates low enough to be acceptable?
- Are people properly trained and supported?
- Are there sufficient confident and skilled people?
- What further is needed to support success?
- How will problems be addressed?
- How did the outcome compare to the original plan?
- How satisfied are your stakeholders? If you don't know, find out.
- Were the needs of the end-users met?
- Is the project sponsor satisfied?

- What has been the impact of the project on the customer?

### Identify areas for further development

- Have all of the benefits been achieved? If not, what is needed to achieve them?
- Is there any further training and coaching that could maximise results?
- Could you make any additional changes that would deliver even more value?
- Are there any other benefits that can be achieved?
- How could you harness those additional benefits?

### Identify lessons learned

- How did the project deliver?
- Did you keep to the agreed timescale and budgeted costs?
- What went wrong, and how could these problems be avoided in future?
- What went well and needs to be replicated in future?

### Report findings and recommendations

- What have you learned?
- Do you need to undertake any corrective action to get the benefits you want?
- What lessons have you learned that need to be carried forward to future projects?

## TOOL: THE SMERTIE GOAL FRAMEWORK FOR CREATING HIGH-QUALITY GOALS

Many people are familiar with SMART goals;[152] SMART goals are too mechanical for a Maslow, self-actualised organisation. SMERTIE is the mnemonic acronym that Andrea uses in her master coach practice. This should be used for all of your goals, eg health, family and relationships. We are more than just working beings, which brings us back to Maslow. SMERTIE stands for:

- Specific – For your goal to have meaning and relevance it must be very clearly defined.

- Measurable – A goal with specific criteria which measures your progress towards accomplishing it.

- Evidential – You need to be able to show practical evidence that you can achieve this goal.

- Responsibility – An effective goal is one that demands that you take full responsibility for taking the action required to manifest it.

- Timed – The goals that you set must have a specific date or timeline by which you intend to achieve them.

- Inspirational – Your goal should inspire you. Ideally, it is there to help you get to self-actualisation. The more inspired you are, the closer you are to achieve Maslow's highest pinnacle of the hierarchy of needs.

- Emotion – Goals are about moving forward and growth, and feeling, knowing and thinking that you are on the right path.

## TOOL: SCHEDULE YOUR GOALS INTO A TO-DO CALENDAR

The to-do list is not as good as it's cracked up to be. People write and rewrite to-do lists each day with the same ten, twenty or thirty items that they then cross off today's list and carry forward, with varying degrees of discipline, to the next day. Does this sound familiar? Thanks to the daily stream of conversations, memos, messages and emails, new things are continually being added to the list and older items are not getting crossed off. It can be difficult to distinguish between priorities; even if each task is allocated a priority level, this tends to be an arbitrary exercise, although a modified use of the risk matrix introduced in Pathway 6 can help formalise this prioritisation process – 'What is the risk if I don't do this task today?' The trouble is, there is no action-guiding time dimension to the to-do list.

The good news is that a better way exists, and it's simple! As your tasks and goals arrive, put them directly into your schedule or diary. Work out how long is required to complete the work, and whether it would be better done in one go or as a series of smaller attempts; then note the deadline. With those two bits of information, you can now block out an appropriate amount of time in your schedule to work your way to meeting your deadline. This approach can be applied to tasks of all sizes. You will gain great peace of mind from knowing that all your important work is scheduled into your calendar.

Moving your to-do list to a to-do calendar is incredibly cathartic. At any point in any day, you know what you need to be working on. There's no longer any need to worry about missing a deadline as this has all been built into the schedule, and this frees up space in your mind that was previously occupied by the fear of missing deadlines. It helps when new work comes in: you can already see how full your week is because you've already mapped what you need to do into your schedule, along with the time needed for each activity. When asked to take on additional tasks, you are now in a position to confidently assess your ability to complete them, accepting if you can but also refusing if necessary: 'Thank you for asking. Looking at my schedule, I have no more than two and a half hours free this week so let's see what can be done in the available time. I may not be able to do it all, so perhaps you can break it down and get others involved if necessary?' This makes clear that you control your schedule and set realistic expectations about your ability to deliver before committing to taking on the new piece of work.

Making this a team habit will make you more consistent goal setters and goal achievers, reducing overall team stress and near eliminating nondelivery of agreed goals.

---

## TOOL: THE OGSM METHODOLOGY TO DEFINE, ALIGN AND CASCADE GOALS

OGSM is an acronym for objectives, goals, strategies and measures, and is a commonly used tool used in goal setting and planning contexts as a framework by which to turn plans and visions into action.[153] OGSM has been popularised by its use in many blue-chip household name companies, including P&G, Coca-Cola and many Fortune 500 companies, but you don't have to be a corporate behemoth to use it; it is a valuable tool whatever your size.[154]

Let's go through each component in turn.

- The **objective** is 'a *qualitative* statement about your ambition.... It is the destination of your journey.' It sets out to answer the fundamental question: 'What are we trying to achieve?' It is important to remember that this is not an organisation's vision or mission, which have a longer time horizon; the objective is bound to a period of just one to five years.

- **Goals** provide 'the *quantitative* description of your objective' and 'translate your qualitative objective statement into measurable figures.' Return to the SMERTIE model for further guidance on setting these goals.

- **Strategies** are the key initiatives you undertake to realise your objective and achieve your goals. They outline the journey to reach the destination defined in the objective. 'Strategies are the qualitative description of your roadmap to success.'

- 'The **measures** describe the concrete action plan and metrics for each strategy. Measures quantify the strategies and clarify who does what by when.'[155] These are the KPI, the metrics by which you will assess whether or not you have been successful.

### How to use the OGSM framework

1. To kick off the planning process using this framework, the senior project leader publicly outlines their OGSMs, guided by the organisation's purpose, mission and vision.

   There can be a tendency at first simply to list the key projects and initiatives, but it's important also to discuss why these points have made the list. What was the logic for these initiatives? Why were they important? How did they fit with the organisation's vision, mission and purpose? This takes the thinking up a level.

2. After the leader has explained their OGSMs to the team, the direct report then steps up.

   As you can see from this diagram, the leader's strategy becomes the team member's objective; their measures became the direct report's goals. The direct report then adds their strategies and measures. If necessary, this exercise can then be repeated a third time if there's another level present, using the direct report's strategies and measures to generate their objectives and goals.

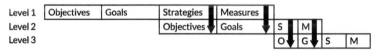

3. Now that you have aligned the OGSMs across all levels, compare the OGSM list with each team member's current 'to do' list. How much time is spent on these critical activities? The answer can be a shock – it might be less than half.

4. To fix this, decide what activities should be stopped (or at least suspended) and which activities could be delegated. This will require some difficult conversations and some adjustment of expectations as the team lays down some of their activities and others are expected to pick them up. It's much easier to have these difficult conversations if you can refer to the aligned OGSMs and demonstrate how these 'legacy' activities are not connected to these high-value-aligned goals.

Employing the OGSM framework is a truly productive way to sharpen and align goals within a team.

## Consistency and Conformity: Three questions

| | |
|---|---|
| *People* | Do you consistently set realistic, relevant and clear goals? |
| *Task* | Does the team focus on making consistent decisions? |
| *System* | Are your projects attentive to the consequences of your solutions for the organisation's global community and external stakeholders? |

## Summary

In this chapter, we looked at the final of the nine pathways, Pathway 9: Consistency and Conformity. Having built a good culture through each of the previous eight pathways, we considered ways in which you could ensure your culture remained consistent and aligned throughout the organisation, and we provided many tools to help.

# Conclusion

Congratulations, you've completed all nine pathways necessary to develop and maintain a good culture! You have learned all the necessary steps and discovered their importance. If you do not work through each of the pathways in sequence, your goal will fail, so now you need to return to Pathway 1: Trust and begin the process of implementing it in your workplace. Once you have completed Pathway 1, move on to Pathway 2, and keep going until you complete each of the nine pathways in your organisation. We have provided tools to help you along the way. This book provides a great starting point. However if you are serious about creating your good culture, then you should go further and explore the Axiometrics® tools and services. They will enable you to define your culture blueprint, measure your team's current thinking capacities and ability to access their talent, and give you a roadmap for development and to measure the distance travelled. Do not underestimate the importance of this process. Good cultures equip organisations to weather the storms, deliver strong performances and generate healthy and happy workers with the resilience and determination to match.

Now, perhaps more than ever before, we live in a VUCA world. The pandemic caused a radical reimagining of how businesses could, and should, operate; in response, significant changes came about that would have seemed almost unimaginable a year before. The shift towards virtual and hybrid working models is an example of such a change and it is one that seems likely to remain for many years to come. However, as the global pandemic demonstrated all too well, we must always expect the unexpected. You cannot hope to plan for the unexpected, but you should plan with the anticipation of *something* unforeseen occurring. It is impossible to know what lies in wait for us around the corner so expecting yourself to produce strategies and plans to deal with all possible eventualities in any number of unknown scenarios is unrealistic. Instead you need to ensure that leaders and their teams are enabled with the ability to adapt – sometimes overnight – to manage the unexpected. A good culture, underpinned by correctly aligned core values, behaviours and beliefs, makes this level of agility possible, with organisations able to respond to change with adaptation, resilience, innovation and creativity.

You might still feel overwhelmed by the challenge of building a good culture. That's understandable but remember that this shift is not something that needs to be done overnight. If you work through the pathways, you will be conferring on your organisation the flexibility and resilience required to respond immediately to change of any sort, but generating this ability requires a significant cultural change, and these movements take time. This shouldn't put you off: consider the Chinese proverb ascribed to Laozi, 'A journey of a thousand miles begins with a single step.'[156]

In this book, we have provided a guide to those first steps. We designed it as a 'how to' guide, and you should take it with you along the journey. We recommend that you begin by returning to the first pathway and focus only on the first step, building trust. This first step is, in many ways, the most important: the journey to a good culture will never succeed if you do not set out correctly. Trust is the currency of good teams and organisations. It fosters the willingness to co-operate and makes collaboration happen; it is essential for positive working relationships because it is central to engaging with each other. When trust is in place, people willingly contribute what is needed and more, not just by turning up, but by offering their dedication, talent, energy and ideas. Communication becomes transparent and unimpaired as colleagues thrive in an honest and supportive environment of mutual respect and shared purpose; in contrast, teams can't function well when colleagues can't trust one another.

We wrote this book for leaders. The change starts with you and if you don't take the time to stop and consider who you need to be as a leader, then it's unlikely that you will take people with you. As you will have noted, we provided a section within each chapter on who you need to be as a leader in order to develop and implement the pathways most successfully. Put aside some time to think these qualities through thoroughly and consider how you can strengthen your performance in these areas. A good culture requires good leadership.

If you are not yet ready to embark upon a culture- change journey, there is still much you can take from this book. If we have only one piece of advice for you, it would be to look at any given scenario and consider your decision through Hartman's three dimensions of value. Before acting on anything, take a moment to ask yourself three questions:

| | |
|---|---|
| *People* | 'What are the implications for our people?' |
| *Task* | 'What are the practical implications of this?' |
| *System* | 'How does it fit with the rules and our longer-term plans?' |

If you'd like to learn more or take an online thinking exercise designed to help you understand how you think and make decisions using the three dimensions of value, you can find out more by visiting our website, where you will also find additional resources. Should you want more support for your workplace, we work with a few organisations each year in our consultancy and we would be pleased to accompany you through your change journey. It all starts with a conversation and our contact details are provided at the end of the book.

All organisations should have good cultures. We wish you every success as you set about building a good culture for your organisation, aligning your people, profits and purpose for the greater good.

---

### TOOL: GOOD CULTURE SCORECARD

 You can get a free snapshot of your culture by taking our good culture scorecard. It will give you an instant risk assessment of the health of your culture (high/low or medium). You can then dive deeper with our second scorecard to help you diagnose the pain points that may be damaging your culture. Scan the QR code or follow the link: *https://good-culture.scoreapp.com*

---

We have provided inspiration, ideas, tools and the road-map to help you achieve this success, and now we pass it over to you as you take that first step on this journey. We are truly excited to see what you will achieve and the culture you will create. Let us know how you get on.

# Notes

1   'Volatility, uncertainty, complexity and ambiguity', Wikipedia
    (last edited December 2021), https://en.wikipedia.org/wiki/
    Volatility,_uncertainty,_complexity_and_ambiguity, accessed
    February 2022

2   B Groysberg et al, 'Leader's guide to corporate culture: How
    to manage the eight critical elements of organizational life',
    *Harvard Business Review* (January–February 2018), https://hbr.
    org/2018/01/the-leaders-guide-to-corporate-culture, accessed
    February 2022

3   EH Schein et al, *Organizational Culture and Leadership: A dynamic
    view* (Jossey-Bass, 1985)

4   TE Deal and AA Kennedy, *Corporate Cultures: The rites and rituals
    of corporate life* (Penguin Books, 1982; reissue Perseus Books,
    2000); cited at 'Organizational culture', Wikipedia (last edited
    February 2022), https://en.wikipedia.org/wiki/Organizational_
    culture, accessed February 2022

5   B Jaruzelski, J Loehr and R Holman, 'The Global Innovation
    1000: Why innovation is key', *strategy+business*, 65 (Winter 2011),
    Reprint 11404, 1–18, 3, www.strategy-business.com//media/
    file/sb65-11404-Global-Innovation-1000-Why-Culture-Is-Key.pdf,
    accessed February 2022

6   A DiLeonardo, RL Phelps and B Weddle, 'Establish a performance culture as your "secret sauce": Five actions can lead to effective change' (McKinsey & Company, 27 July 2020), www.mckinsey.com/business-functions/people-and-organizational-performance/our-insights/the-organization-blog/establish-a-performance-culture-as-your-secret-sauce, accessed February 2022

7   B Ewenstein, W Smith and A Sologar, 'Changing change management' (McKinsey & Company, 1 July 2015), www.mckinsey.com/featured-insights/leadership/changing-change-management, accessed February 2022

8   Financial Reporting Council, 'The UK Corporate Governance Code' (Financial Reporting Council, July 2018), 1–20, www.frc.org.uk/getattachment/88bd8c45-50ea-4841-95b0-d2f4f48069a2/2018-UK-Corporate-Governance-Code-FINAL.PDF, accessed February 2022

9   D Campbell, D Edgar and G Stonehouse, *Business Strategy: An introduction* (Palgrave Macmillan, 2011; 3rd edition), 263

10  E Hoffman, *The Right To Be Human: A biography of Abraham Maslow* (McGraw Hill, 1999), 7

11  The Robert S Hartman Institute, www.hartmaninstitute.org/life-of-robert-s-hartman, accessed February 2022

12  RS Hartman and CG Hurst, *The Revolution Against War: Selected writings on war and peace* (Izzard Ink, 2020)

13  RS Hartman, *Freedom to Live: The Robert Hartman story*, edited by AR Ellis (1994; 2nd edition, Wipf and Stock Publishers, 2013)

14  C Hurst, 'Maslow: a psychologist; Hartman: a philosopher; you: a conference attendee' (Association for Humanistic Psychology, 21 October 2020), https://ahpweb.org/maslow-a-psychologist-hartman-a-philosopher-you-a-conference-attendee, accessed February 2022

15  RS Hartman, *The Structure of Value: Foundations of scientific axiology* (Southern Illinois University Press, 1967), 22

16  The Robert S. Hartman Institute, 'About the Institute' (The Robert S. Hartman Institute, no date), www.hartmaninstitute.org, accessed February 2022

17  V Govindarajan and AK Gupta, 'Building an effective global business team', *IEEE Engineering Management Review*, 30/2 (2002), 28, https://doi.org/10.1109/EMR.2002.1022419

18  ME Turner and AR Pratkanis, 'Twenty-five years of groupthink theory and research: Lessons from the evaluation of a theory', *Organizational Behavior and Human Decision Processes* , 73/2–3 (1998), 105–115

19 PB Viall, *Managing as a Performing Art: New ideas for a world of chaotic change* (Jossey-Bass, 1989)

20 Gartner for HR, 'Top five priorities for HR leaders in 2022: Actionable and objective advice to tackle top HR challenges' (Gartner, October 2021), 1–24, 8, https://emtemp.gcom.cloud/ngw/globalassets/en/human-resources/documents/trends/top-priorities-for-hr-leaders-2022.pdf, accessed February 2022

21 B Johansen, *Leaders Make the Future: Ten new leadership skills for an uncertain world* (2009; 2nd edition, Berrett-Koehler Publishers, 2012), 18

22 AH Maslow, 'A theory of human motivation', *Psychological Review*, 50/4 (1943), 370–396, https://motivationalmagic.com/library/ebooks/motivation/maslow_a-theory-of-human-motivation.pdf, accessed February 2022

23 AH Maslow, *Religions, Values and Peak-experiences* (1964; 2nd edition, Penguin, 1976)

24 WC Kim and R Mauborgne, *Blue Ocean Strategy: How to create uncontested market space and make the competition irrelevant* (2004; 2nd edition, Harvard Business Review Press, 2015)

25 K Morgan, 'Why introverts excelled at working from home' (BBC, 16 July 2021) www.bbc.com/worklife/article/20210713-why-introverts-excelled-at-working-from-home, accessed March 2022

26 M Johanson, 'Hybrid work: How "proximity bias" can lead to favouritism' (BBC, 9 August 2021), www.bbc.com/worklife/article/20210804-hybrid-work-how-proximity-bias-can-lead-to-favouritism, accessed February 2022

27 Gartner, 'Gartner top three priorities for HR leaders in 2021' (Gartner, 23 October 2020), www.gartner.com/smarterwithgartner/gartner-top-3-priorities-for-hr-leaders-in-2021, accessed February 2022

28 S Blinkhorn and C Johnson, 'The insignificance of personality testing', *Nature*, 348 (20/27 December 1990), 671–672, 672, www.catapult-solutions.co.uk/wp-content/uploads/2020/04/Blinkhorn-Johnson1990_Article_TheInsignificanceOfPersonality-002.pdf, accessed February 2022

29 W Isaacson, 'The real leadership lessons of Steve Jobs', *Harvard Business Review* (April 2012), https://hbr.org/2012/04/the-real-leadership-lessons-of-steve-jobs, accessed February 2022

30 PricewaterhouseCoopers, 'It's time to reimagine where and how work will get done: PwC's US remote work survey' (PricewaterhouseCoopers, 12 January 2021), www.pwc.com/us/en/library/covid-19/us-remote-work-survey.html, accessed February 2022

31  E Azer, 'Remote working has led to managers spying more on staff – here are three ways to curb it', *The Conversation* (6 May 2021), https://theconversation.com/remote-working-has-led-to-managers-spying-more-on-staff-here-are-three-ways-to-curb-it-159604, accessed February 2022
    K Ball, 'Electronic monitoring and surveillance in the workplace' (European Commission, 2021), https://publications.jrc.ec.europa.eu/repository/handle/JRC125716

32  'Axiology', *Encyclopedia Britannica* (10 June 2015), www.britannica.com/topic/axiology, accessed February 2022

33  RS Hartman, *The Structure of Value: Foundations of scientific axiology* (Southern Illinois University Press, 1967), 22

34  'Formal Axiology', Clear Direction Inc, www.cleardirection.com/docs/formalaxiology.asp, accessed March 2022

35  'Science of values', Wikipedia (last edited December 2018), https://en.wikipedia.org/wiki/Science_of_value, accessed February 2022

36  B Hancock, B Schaninger and B Weddle, 'Culture in the hybrid workplace', McKinsey & Company podcast (11 June 2021), www.mckinsey.com/business-functions/people-and-organizational-performance/our-insights/culture-in-the-hybrid-workplace, accessed February 2022

37  M Bucy, S Hall and D Yakola, 'Transformation with a capital *T*', *McKinsey Quarterly* (7 November 2016), www.mckinsey.com/business-functions/rts/our-insights/transformation-with-a-capital-t, accessed February 2022

38  T Basford and B Schaninger, 'The four building blocks of change', *McKinsey Quarterly* (11 April 2016), www.mckinsey.com/business-functions/people-and-organizational-performance/our-insights/the-four-building-blocks--of-change, accessed February 2022

39  AH Maslow, 'A theory of human motivation', *Psychological Review*, 50/4 (July 1943), 370–396, http://citeseerx.ist.psu.edu/viewdoc/download?doi=10.1.1.318.2317&rep=rep1&type=pdf, accessed February 2022

40  AH Maslow, *Motivation and Personality* (Harper & Brothers, 1954)

41  AH Maslow, 'A theory of human motivation', *Psychological Review*, 50/4 (July 1943), 370–396, 383, http://citeseerx.ist.psu.edu/viewdoc/download?doi=10.1.1.318.2317&rep=rep1&type=pdf, accessed February 2022

42  AH Maslow, *The Farther Reaches of Human Nature* (Penguin, 1971), 4

43  AH Maslow, *Religions, Values, and Peak-experiences* (1964; 2nd edition, Penguin, 1976)

44  AH Maslow, 'The farther reaches of human nature', *Journal of Transpersonal Psychology*, 1/1 (1969), 1–9, https://psycnet.apa.org/record/1970-17664-001, accessed February 2022

45  AH Maslow, *Toward a Psychology of Being* (1962; Martino Fine Books, reprint of 1st edition, 2010), 74

46  RS Hartman, *Freedom to Live: The Robert Hartman story*, edited by AR Ellis (1994; 2nd edition, Wipf & Stock Publishers, 2013), 4

47  Axiometrics® Partners, 'Axiometrics® Validity Studies' (Axiometrics International, Inc., 2019), 6, www.catapult-solutions.co.uk/wp-content/uploads/2019/10/Axiometrics%E2%84%A2-Validity-Studies-prepared-by-Axiometrics-International-Inc-revised-2019.pdf, accessed February 2022

48  R Davies, 'A little-known tool to make coaches more effective' (Catapult Solutions, no date), www.catapult-solutions.co.uk/a-little-known-tool-to-make-coaches-more-effective, accessed February 2022

49  Axiometrics International, www.axiometrics.net

50  KT Connor, 'Assessing organizational ethics: Measuring the gaps', *Industrial and Commercial Training*, 38/3 (2006), 148–155, https://doi.org/10.1108/00197850610659418

51  KT Connor, 'Assessing organizational ethics: Measuring the gaps', *Industrial and Commercial Training*, 38/3 (2006), 148–155, https://doi.org/10.1108/00197850610659418

52  'faking', *APA Dictionary of Psychology* (American Psychological Association, no date), https://dictionary.apa.org/faking, accessed February 2022

53  P Kline, *Handbook of Psychological Testing* (1993; 2nd edition, Routledge, 1999)

54  E Andrews, 'What was the Gordian knot?' (*Sky HISTORY*, 3 February 2016; 29 August 2018), www.history.com/news/what-was-the-gordian-knot, accessed February 2022

55  R Hougaard, 'The power of putting people first', (*Forbes*, 2019), www.forbes.com/sites/rasmushougaard/2019/03/05/the-power-of-putting-people-first/

56  P Tréguer, 'Meaning and origin of "To take the (King's/Queen's) shilling"' (Word Histories, 16 October 2017), https://wordhistories.net/2017/10/16/kings-shilling-origin, accessed February 2022

57  Windows Phone timeline, https://mobiforge.com/timeline/windows-phone-history, accessed March 2022

58   L Mearian, 'Yes, Windows Phone is dead. Here's why',
     *Computerworld* (2017), accessed April 2022 www.computerworld.
     com/article/3231985/yes-windows-phone-is-dead-heres-why.
     html

59   Axiometrics® Partners, 'Axiometrics® Validity Studies'
     (Axiometrics International, Inc., 2019), www.catapult-solutions.
     co.uk/wp-content/uploads/2019/10/Axiometrics%E2%84%A2-
     Validity-Studies-prepared-by-Axiometrics-International-Inc-
     revised-2019.pdf, accessed April 2022

60   'Harold Shipman', Wikipedia (last edited February 2022),
     https://en.wikipedia.org/wiki/Harold_Shipman, accessed
     February 2022

61   'SWOT analysis', Wikipedia (last edited January 2022), https://
     en.wikipedia.org/wiki/SWOT_analysis, accessed February 2022

62   'Synergy', *Online Etymology Dictionary* (no date), www.
     etymonline.com/search?q=synergy, accessed February 2022

63   'Superficial', *Online Etymology Dictionary* (no date), www.
     etymonline.com/word/superficial, accessed February 2022

64   C Duhigg, *The Power of Habit* (Random House, 2012), xvi

65   Gerald Zaltman, *How Customers Think: Essential insights into the
     mind of the market* (Harvard Business School Press, 2003), www.
     magnatar.nl/Magnatar/Brain_food/Artikelen/2011/8/18_
     Marketing_Metaphoria_-_Zaltman_files/howcustomersthink.
     pdf, accessed March 2022

66   E Donchin, cited by D Goleman, 'New view of mind
     gives unconscious an expanded role', *The New York Times*
     (7 February 1984), www.nytimes.com/1984/02/07/science/
     new-view-of-mind-gives-unconscious-an-expanded-role.html,
     accessed February 2022

67   R Davies, 'Commitment Conversations', GPS Goaltrak Get
     on Trak blog (13 January 2018), www.gpsgoaltrak.com/
     commitment-conversations-increase-accountability-and-
     performance, accessed February 2022

68   IKEA, 'The IKEA vision and values' (IKEA, no date),
     www.ikea.com/gb/en/this-is-ikea/about-us/the-ikea-vision-
     and-values-pub9aa779d0, accessed February 2022

69   Axiometrics Partners, 'Axiometrics Validity Studies' (Axiometrics
     International, Inc., 2019), 6, www.catapult-solutions.co.uk/wp-
     content/uploads/2019/10/Axiometrics%E2%84%A2-Validity-
     Studies-prepared-by-Axiometrics-International-Inc-revised-2019.
     pdf, accessed February 2022

70   RS Hartman, *Freedom to Live: The Robert Hartman story*, edited by
     AR Ellis (1994; 2nd edition, Wipf and Stock Publishers, 2013), 4

71 TE Deal and AA Kennedy, *Corporate Cultures: The rites and rituals of corporate life* (Penguin, 1982; reissue Perseus Books, 2000); cited at 'Organizational culture', Wikipedia (last edited February 2022), https://en.wikipedia.org/wiki/Organizational_culture, accessed February 2022

72 Axiometrics® Partners, 'Axiometrics® leadership screen with nine pathways' (Catapult Solutions, no date), www.catapult-solutions.co.uk/wp-content/uploads/2020/08/Leadership-Screen-with-Nine-Pathways-1.pdf, accessed May 2022

73 D Campbell, D Edgar and G Stonehouse, *Business Strategy: An introduction* (Palgrave Macmillan, 2011; 3rd edition), 263

74 'Responsibility', *Cambridge English Dictionary* (no date), https://dictionary.cambridge.org/dictionary/english/responsibility, accessed February 2022

75 'Integrity', *Cambridge English Dictionary* (no date), https://dictionary.cambridge.org/dictionary/english/integrity, accessed February 2022

76 'Tony Dungy quote', Libquotes.com (no date), https://libquotes.com/tony-dungy/quote/lbb4o4w, accessed February 2022

77 'Accountability', *Cambridge English Dictionary* (no date), https://dictionary.cambridge.org/dictionary/english/accountability, accessed February 2022

78 Gallup, 'State of the Global Workplace: 2021 Report' (Gallup, 28 June 2021), www.gallup.com/workplace/349484/state-of-the-global-workplace.aspx, accessed February 2022

79 G O'Toole, 'Be the change you wish to see in the world' (Quote Investigator, 23 October 2017), https://quoteinvestigator.com/2017/10/23/be-change, accessed February 2022

80 T Simons, *The Integrity Dividend: Leading by the power of your word* (Jossey-Bass, 2008), 79

81 'RACI Matrix', CIO Wiki (last edited 22 April 2021), https://cio-wiki.org/wiki/RACI_Matrix#cite_note-1, accessed February 2022

82 T Simons, *The Integrity Dividend: Leading by the power of your word* (Jossey-Bass, 2008), 79, 83, 85, 87, 88

83 R Kaplan and D Norton, 'The balanced scorecard: Measures that drive performance', *Harvard Business Review* (January–February 1992), www.hbs.edu/faculty/Pages/item.aspx?num=9161, accessed February 2022

84 J Collins and JI Porras, 'BHAG: Big hairy audacious goal' (Jim Collins, no date), www.jimcollins.com/article_topics/articles/BHAG.html, accessed February 2022

85  K Miller, 'The triple bottom line: What it is & why it's important' (Harvard Business School Online, 8 December 2020), https://online.hbs.edu/blog/post/what-is-the-triple-bottom-line, accessed February 2022

86  B Šandala, 'The forgotten truth about the Moonshot Goal', *Product Coalition* (26 December 2020), https://productcoalition.com/the-forgotten-truth-about-the-moonshot-goal-cf546b344c92, accessed February 2022

87  'Gantt chart', Wikipedia (last edited February 2022), https://en.wikipedia.org/wiki/Gantt_chart, accessed February 2022

88  Axiometrics® Partners, 'Axiometrics® Personal Value Analysis' (Catapult Solutions, August 2020), 1–13, 6, www.catapult-solutions.co.uk/wp-content/uploads/2020/08/Personal-Value-Analysis.pdf, accessed February 2022

89  W Chai, 'Eisenhower Matrix' (WhatIs.com, no date), https://whatis.techtarget.com/definition/Eisenhower-Matrix, accessed February 2022. Also S Covey, *The 7 Habits of Highly Effective People: Powerful lessons in personal change* (Free Press, 1989), https://resources.franklincovey.com/the-7-habits-of-highly-effective-people/habit-5- seek-first-to-understand-then-to-be-understood, accessed February 2022

90  G O'Toole, 'What is important is seldom urgent and what is urgent is seldom important' (Quote Investigator, 9 May 2015), https://quoteinvestigator.com/2014/05/09/urgent, accessed February 2022

91  GPS Goaltrak, 'How to prioritise – Urgent vs important', GPS Goaltrak Get on Trak blog (21 March 2018), www.gpsgoaltrak.com/how-to-prioritise, accessed February 2022

92  'Definitions for sales competencies' (Catapult Solutions, no date), 1–3, 3, www.catapult-solutions.co.uk/wp-content/uploads/2019/10/20160217-Definitions-For-Sales-Competencies.pdf, accessed February 2022

93  'Prayer of Saint Francis', Wikipedia (last edited February 2022), https://en.wikipedia.org/wiki/Prayer_of_Saint_Francis, accessed February 2022

94  S Covey, *The 7 Habits of Highly Effective People: Powerful lessons in personal change* (Free Press, 1989), https://resources.franklincovey.com/the-7-habits-of-highly-effective-people/habit-5-seek-first-to-understand-then-to-be-understood, accessed February 2022

95  R Burns, 'To a Mouse: On turning up in her nest with a plough, November, 1785', www.scottishpoetrylibrary.org.uk/poem/mouse, accessed February 2022

96   G O'Toole, 'No plan survives first contact with the enemy' (Quote Investigator, 4 May 2021), https://quoteinvestigator. com/2021/05/04/no-plan, accessed February 2022

97   VUCA World, 'Leadership skills and strategies: VUCA world' (VUCA-WORLD, no date), www.vuca-world.org, accessed February 2022

98   C Duhigg, *The Power of Habit* (Random House, 2012), xvi

99   VUCA World, 'Leadership skills and strategies: VUCA world' (VUCA-WORLD, no date), www.vuca-world.org, accessed February 2022

100   'Innovation', *Online Etymology Dictionary* (no date), www. etymonline.com/search?q=innovation, accessed February 2022

101   'Change', *Online Etymology Dictionary* (no date), www. etymonline.com/search?q=change, accessed February 2022

102   'Change', *Cambridge English Dictionary* (no date), https:// dictionary.cambridge.org/dictionary/english/change, accessed February 2022

103   SD Anthony et al, 'Breaking down the barriers to innovation: Build the habits and routines that lead to growth', (*Harvard Business Review* (November–December 2019), https://hbr. org/2019/11/breaking-down-the-barriers-to-innovation, accessed February 2022

104   B Jaruzelski, J Loehr and R Holman, 'The Global Innovation 1000: Why innovation is key', *strategy+business*, 65 (Winter 2011), Reprint 11404, 1–18, 4, www.strategy-business.com//media/ file/sb65-11404-Global-Innovation-1000-Why-Culture-Is-Key.pdf, accessed February 2022

105   K Goetz, 'How 3M gave everyone days off and created an innovation dynamo', *Fast Company* (2 January 2011), www. fastcompany.com/1663137/how-3m-gave-everyone-days-off- and-created-an-innovation-dynamo, accessed February 2022

106   'Fail-fast', Wikipedia (last edited January 2022), https:// en.wikipedia.org/wiki/Fail-fast, accessed February 2022

107   R Black, 'Glossophobia (Fear of Public Speaking): Are you glossophobic?' (Psycom.net, no date), www.psycom.net/ glossophobia-fear-of-public-speaking, accessed February 2022

108   'Formula for change', Wikipedia (last edited January 2022), https://en.wikipedia.org/wiki/Formula_for_change, accessed February 2022

109   D Gleicher, published in R Beckhard and RT Harris, *Organizational Transitions: Managing complex change* (Addison- Wesley, 1977; 2nd edition, 1987)

110   KD Dannemiller and RW Jacobs, 'Changing the way
        organizations change: A revolution of common sense', *The Journal
        of Applied Behavioral Science*, 28/4 (1 December 1992), 480–498,
        https://doi.org/10.1177/0021886392284003, cited at 'Formula for
        change', Wikipedia

111   'Prepare', *Cambridge English Dictionary* (no date), https://
        dictionary.cambridge.org/dictionary/english/prepare, accessed
        February 2022

112   'Prepare', *Online Etymology Dictionary* (no date), www.
        etymonline.com/word/prepare, accessed February 2022

113   'Tactics', *Online Etymology Dictionary* (no date), www.etymonline.
        com/search?q=tactics, accessed February 2022

114   'Tactic', *Cambridge English Dictionary* (no date), https://
        dictionary.cambridge.org/dictionary/english/tactic, accessed
        February 2022

115   G O'Toole, 'No plan survives first contact with the enemy'
        (Quote Investigator, 4 May 2021), https://quoteinvestigator.
        com/2021/05/04/no-plan, accessed February 2022

116   '7 Ps (military adage)', Military Wiki (last edited July 2021),
        https://military-history.fandom.com/wiki/7_Ps_(military_
        adage), accessed February 2022

117   LA Liswood, *The Loudest Duck: Moving beyond diversity while
        embracing differences to achieve success at work* (John Wiley & Sons
        Inc., 2009)

118   'Sakichi Toyoda', Lean Six Sigma Definition (no date), www.
        leansixsigmadefinition.com/glossary/sakichi-toyoda, accessed
        February 2022

119   T Ohno, *Toyota Production System: Beyond large-scale production*
        (Productivity Press, 1988, 3rd edition), 263

120   'Likert scale', Wikipedia (last edited February 2022),
        https://en.wikipedia.org/wiki/Likert_scale, accessed
        February 2022

121   'Constancy', *Cambridge English Dictionary* (no date), https://
        dictionary.cambridge.org/dictionary/english/constancy,
        accessed February 2022

122   'Conformity', *Online Etymology Dictionary* (no date), www.
        etymonline.com/search?q=conformity, accessed February 2022

123   'Conformity', *Cambridge English Dictionary* (no date), https://
        dictionary.cambridge.org/dictionary/english/conformity,
        accessed February 2022

124  B Jaruzelski, J Loehr and R Holman, 'The Global Innovation
     1000: Why innovation is key', *strategy+business*, 65 (Winter 2011),
     Reprint 11404, 1–18, 4, www.strategy-business.com//media/
     file/sb65-11404-Global-Innovation-1000-Why-Culture-Is-Key.pdf,
     accessed February 2022

125  'Conditional sentence', Wikipedia (last edited January 2022),
     https://en.wikipedia.org/wiki/Conditional_sentence, accessed
     February 2022

126  JA Rodriguez, 'Consequential leadership: The key to a safe
     landing', *EHS Today* (8 November 2016), www.ehstoday.com/
     safety/article/21918337/consequential-leadership-the-key-to-a-
     safe-landing, accessed February 2022

127  'European Union competition law', Wikipedia (last edited
     January 2022), https://en.wikipedia.org/wiki/European_
     Union_competition_law, accessed February 2022

128  A Woolich, 'A guide to EU Commission fines' (HFW
     Publications, September 2012), www.hfw.com/A-Guide-to-EU-
     Commission-Fines-Sept-2012, accessed February 2022

129  European Commission, 'Antitrust: Commission fines Google
     €2.42 billion for abusing dominance as search engine by
     giving illegal advantage to own comparison shopping service'
     (European Commission, 27 June 2017), https://ec.europa.eu/
     commission/presscorner/detail/en/memo_17_1785, accessed
     February 2022

130  European Commission, 'Antitrust: Commission fines Google
     €4.34 billion for illegal practices regarding Android mobile
     devices to strengthen dominance of Google's search engine'
     (European Commission, 18 July 2018), https://ec.europa.eu/
     commission/presscorner/detail/en/IP_18_4581, accessed
     February 2022

131  European Commission, 'Antitrust: Commission fines Google
     €1.49 billion for abusive practices in online advertising'
     (European Commission, 20 March 2019), https://ec.europa.
     eu/commission/presscorner/detail/en/IP_19_1770, accessed
     February 2022

132  European Commission, 'Antitrust: Commission fines truck
     producers € 2.93 billion for participating in a cartel' (European
     Commission, 19 July 2016), https://ec.europa.eu/commission/
     presscorner/detail/es/IP_16_2582, accessed February 2022

133  A Shalchi, 'The UK competition regime', Briefing paper to
     the House of Commons, number 04814 (Commons Library,
     25 May 2021), https://researchbriefings.files.parliament.uk/
     documents/SN04814/SN04814.pdf, accessed February 2022

134 M Lewis, 'The impact of Brexit on UK Competition Law cases' (JD Supra, 18 March 2021), www.jdsupra.com/legalnews/the-impact-of-brexit-on-uk-competition-7400074, accessed February 2022

135 'General Data Protection Regulation', Wikipedia (last edited February 2022), https://en.wikipedia.org/wiki/General_Data_Protection_Regulation, accessed February 2022

136 IT Governance, 'Data protection and Brexit: How the UK's withdrawal from the EU affects data protection in the UK: the EU GDPR, UK DPA 2018 and UK GDPR' (IT Governance, no date), www.itgovernance.co.uk/eu-gdpr-uk-dpa-2018-uk-gdpr, accessed February 2022

137 IT Governance, 'An overview of UK Data Protection Law: The UK GDPR, DPA 2018 and EU GDPR, and the ePR and PECR' (IT Governance, no date), www.itgovernance.co.uk/data-protection, accessed February 2022

138 B Wolford, 'What are the GDPR Fines?' (GDPR.EU, no date), https://gdpr.eu/fines, accessed February 2022

139 'Anti-bribery policy' (GOV.UK, no date), www.gov.uk/anti-bribery-policy, accessed February 2022

140 'Bribery Act 2010', Commentary on sections, Section 11: Penalties, 56, www.legislation.gov.uk/ukpga/2010/23/section/11, accessed February 2022

141 Colin Ng & Partners, 'UK Bribery Act 2010: Facts and implications for businesses' (CNP Update, 26 January 2012), 1–3, 2, https://cnplaw.com/cnpupdate/Media/Content/Articles/2012/01/UK%20Bribery%20Act%202010.pdf, accessed February 2022

142 L Morgan, 'Logistics firm pay £2.2m fine after breaching anti-bribery Act' (IT Governance, 4 April 2016), www.itgovernance.co.uk/blog/logistics-firm-pay-2-2m-fine-after-breaching-anti-bribery-act, accessed February 2022

143 Government Equalities Office and Equality and Human Rights Commission, 'Equality Act 2010: Guidance' (last updated June 2015), www.gov.uk/guidance/equality-act-2010-guidance, accessed February 2022

144 'Equality Act 2010: Explanatory notes' (revised August 2010), Commentary on sections, Part 9 (Enforcement), Section 119: Remedies, 389, www.legislation.gov.uk/ukpga/2010/15/notes/division/3/9, accessed February 2022

145 'Public sector Equality Duty' (last updated June 2011), www.gov.uk/guidance/equality-act-2010-guidance#public-sector-equality-duty, accessed February 2022

146 Equality and Human Rights Commission, 'The essential guide to the public sector equality duty' (Equality and Human Rights Commission, 7 January 2014), 34, www.equalityhumanrights. com/en/publication-download/essential-guide-public-sector-equality-duty, accessed February 2022

147 'Terms of reference', *Cambridge English Dictionary* (no date), https://dictionary.cambridge.org/dictionary/english/terms-of-reference, accessed February 2022

148 'Terms of reference', Wikipedia (last edited January 2021), https://en.wikipedia.org/wiki/Terms_of_reference, accessed February

149 E McConnell, 'Project Terms of Reference (TOR) template' (MyManagementGuide.com, 16 March 2012), https:// mymanagementguide.com/terms-of-reference-tor-template, accessed February 2022

150 'Work breakdown structure', Wikipedia (last edited February 2022), https://en.wikipedia.org/wiki/Work_breakdown_ structure, accessed February 2022

151 'Timeboxing', Wikipedia (last edited February 2022), https:// en.wikipedia.org/wiki/Timeboxing, accessed February 2022

152 'SMART criteria', Wikipedia (last edited February 2022), https:// en.wikipedia.org/wiki/SMART_criteria, accessed February 2022

153 'OGSM', Wikipedia (last edited December 2021), https:// en.wikipedia.org/wiki/OGSM, accessed February 2022

154 'What is OGSM?', Rock Your Strategy (no date), https:// rockyourstrategy.com/what-does-ogsm-stand-for, accessed February 2022

155 'What is OGSM?', Rock Your Strategy (no date), https:// rockyourstrategy.com/what-does-ogsm-stand-for, accessed February 2022

156 'A journey of a thousand miles begins with a single step', Wikipedia (last edited February 2022), https://en.wikipedia.org/ wiki/A_journey_of_a_thousand_miles_begins_with_a_single_ step, accessed February 2022

# The Authors

## Andrea Burns

 Andrea Burns is a leadership and productivity expert dedicated to helping organisations such as the MOD, Waitrose, the NHS and small and medium enterprises to make a positive, lasting social impact and create the culture they need to deliver their vision and better outcomes for the people they serve.

# Richard Davies

Richard Davies has extensive experience in corporate commercial roles at Kellogg's and Shell where he discovered his true passion: accelerating the personal development of individuals and improving the effectiveness of teams. He was responsible for the training and development of half a million people in his last corporate role and now coaches people to improve performance, increase focus and accelerate business results.

Catapult Solutions website

 www.catapult-solutions.co.uk

News, publications and fact sheets on our services

 www.catapult-solutions.co.uk/home/ newsandpublications

Catapult Solutions shop

 www.catapult-solutions.co.uk/shop

Lightning Source UK Ltd.
Milton Keynes UK
UKHW021159160622
404525UK00010B/2038